AFRICAN ISSUES

The Criminalization
of the State
in Africa

AFRICAN ISSUES

The Criminalization of the State in Africa

JEAN-FRANÇOIS BAYART
Director CERI, Paris

STEPHEN ELLIS
Afrika-Studiecentrum, Leiden

BÉATRICE HIBOU
CNRS, Bordeaux

Translated from the French
by Stephen Ellis

The International
African Institute
in association with
JAMES CURREY
Oxford
INDIANA UNIVERSITY PRESS
Bloomington & Indianapolis

The International
African Institute
in association with

James Currey
73 Botley Road
Oxford OX2 0BS
&
Indiana University Press
601 North Morton Street
Bloomington
Indiana 47404
(North America)

First published as *La criminalisation de l'état en Afrique* by Editions Complexe, 1997

British Library Cataloguing in Publication Data
Bayart, Jean-Francois
    The Criminalization of the state in Africa. - (African issues)
    1.Crime - Africa
    I.Title II.Ellis, Stephen III.Hibou, Beatrice
    364.1'096

ISBN 0-85255-813-9 (James Currey Cloth)
ISBN 0-85255-812-0 (James Currey Paper)

Library of Congress Cataloging-in-Publication Data
A catalog record for this book is available from the Library of Congress

ISBN 0-253-21286-3 (paper)
ISBN 0-253-33524-8 (cloth)

Typeset by
Saxon Graphics Ltd, Derby
in 9/11 Melior with Optima display

Printed in Great Britain

CONTENTS

LIST OF FIGURES

THE AUTHORS

Jean-François Bayart is a researcher at the Centre national de la recherche scientifique (CNRS) and director of the Centre d'études et de recherches internationales, Paris. Among his most notable books are *L'Etat en Afrique: la politique du ventre* (an English version, entitled *The State in Africa: the Politics of the Belly* was published by Longman in 1993), and *L'Illusion identitaire.* He is director of the *les Afriques* and *Recherches internationales* series published by Éditions Karthala, Paris, and of *Critique internationale,* a review published by Presses de la Fondation nationale des sciences politiques.

Stephen Ellis is a researcher at the Afrika-Studiecentrum in Leiden, the Netherlands, and a former editor of the London-based newsletter *Africa Confidential.* He edited the collection *Africa Now: People, Policies and Institutions,* published by James Currey and Heinemann with the Dutch Ministry of Foreign Affairs (DGIS) in 1996. He is a co-editor of the journal *African Affairs* and of the African Issues series published by James Currey.

Béatrice Hibou is a researcher at the Centre national de la recherche scientifique (CNRS), based at the Centre d'Étude d'Afrique noire, Bordeaux. She is the author of *L'Afrique est-elle protectionniste? Les chemins buissonniers de la libéralisation extérieure,* published by Éditions Karthala, Paris, in 1996.

INTRODUCTION

In June 1995, Alain Juppé, newly appointed as Prime Minister of France, wrote a letter to his colleague Jacques Godfrain, Minister of Co-operation, asking him to take steps to ensure that French development aid should be subordinated to the struggle against crime, corruption and drug trafficking. The tone of this missive, which was unusual in the cloistered world of Franco-African relations, appears to have been connected to an incident described in the newsletter *La lettre du continent*, number 235 of 18 May 1995:

> In the course of a robust exchange of views with Jacques Foccart, accompanied by his deputy Fernand Wibaux, President Chirac, brandishing a confidential report on the criminalization of politics in Africa written by the Policy Planning Unit of the Ministry of Foreign Affairs, informed them that there had to be major changes in Africa policy. The French government had to make a clean break with heads of state who were prevaricating in the face of change, and who were corrupt and autocratic.

Some months later, two more French magazines, *Le canard enchaîné* (27 September 1995) and *Le nouvel observateur* (9 May 1996) published lengthy extracts from a memorandum by the Foreign Ministry's Policy Planning Unit, dated subsequent to Chirac's stormy interview. The document which had so provoked the President's wrath was thus a separate one which had never been leaked to the press. It appears to have contained a warning to the French authorities of the increasing importance of organized crime in countries south of the Sahara and of the growing relationship between crime and tenure of public office. The long-distance forecasting unit at the Quai d'Orsay had in fact been consistently sounding warnings on this subject since 1990. Even at that time, there were signs that authoritarian governments in Africa were taking vigorous counter-measures to halt the advance of democracy, in spite of the impressive size of popular pro-democracy pressures which were sweeping the continent and despite the general spread of multi-party political movements, some of which had actually toppled governments from power.

To some extent the confrontation between senior French politicians and officials represents no more than a footnote to history, since the reform of the system of international co-operation which Juppé hoped to bring about soon faded, and the conduct of France's Africa policy was once more confided to the networks which have traditionally had charge of it.[1] This is one reason, albeit a relatively minor one, why the criminalization of the state in Africa remains a subject of the greatest topical importance.

Deaf to the paeans of the aid donors who saluted the advent of market-based democracies south of the Sahara, celebrated the merits of good governance, praised the virtues of decentralized co-operation and gave an inaugural blessing to an emerging African 'civil society', one researcher at least was more inclined to postulate that events in Africa more closely resembled 'a return to "the heart of darkness"' (Bayart, 1990). This, it was added, 'does not mean a return to "tradition", but rather to a noxious cocktail of commerce and violence, a combination which could be termed, in homage to Siad Barre, "the Somali road to development", were it not that such a description does no justice to the achievements of tenants of power past and present in Sierra Leone and Liberia'. This hypothesis continued as follows:

> In material terms, [this evolution], if it were indeed to be confirmed, appears to be based on the occupation of the most dubious niches of international economic activity (various forms of trafficking, including of drugs; and the dumping of toxic waste, for example) and on the unregulated exploitation of the mineral, oil and wildlife resources of the sub-continent. Politically, it seems to take the form of the radical privatization of the state, the criminalization of the behaviour of power-holders, and even the transformation of factional struggle . . . into armed conflict, as has happened in Chad, Uganda, Angola and Liberia. In cultural terms, it appears to be connected with the re-emergence of representations of the invisible world of spiritual power, often connected with the art of making war. Socially, such a movement appears to be resulting in massive population movements and offering to young school drop-outs, subject in time of peace to adult authority, the possibility of securing access to wealth through means which they themselves see as

[1] We may note that the reform process was resumed by Prime Minister Lionel Jospin in January 1998.

legitimate, a prospect even more enticing than that offered by petty crime. (*ibid.*: 106)

These allusions to Somalia, Liberia and Sierra Leone were justified by the fact that Presidents Barre, Doe and Momoh had advanced very far – perhaps further even than President Mobutu in Zaïre – in the 'politics of dirty tricks', analysed by Joel Migdal in a pioneering work (1988). It was not at all inaccurate to describe their governments as mafias. Only shortly afterwards the Italian press was to reveal the influence wielded by the P2 masonic lodge in Mogadishu, together with that of the Italian chemical industry, anxious to find a dumping ground for its toxic waste through the intermediation of members of the Honourable Society. Giancarlo Parretti experienced his first African adventures in Monrovia, where, until recently, the wreck of one of his aircraft was still visible on the edge of Spriggs-Payne airfield. When Charles Taylor, in those days known as 'Superglue', escaped from an American prison to pursue his ambition of wresting from his former chief Samuel Doe the royalties of the world's largest commercial shipping fleet and the rents to be earned from narco-dollars passing through Liberia thanks to the convertibility of its currency, he offered a stake in the enterprise to Joseph Momoh. President Momoh, whom one might describe as more of a Sierra Loan-er than a Sierra Leonean, promptly offered his services to the highest bidder, which turned out to be Samuel Doe. This whole episode came to a ghastly conclusion, worthy of a second-rate horror movie, with Doe being tortured to death, and the video cassette of his last agony going on popular sale throughout Africa. By early 1997, Taylor had still not realized his political ambition but had succeeded in amassing vast wealth and in punishing Momoh by starting a rebellion in Sierra Leone, which soon provoked Momoh's own overthrow. Sierra Leone and Liberia remained possible sources of contagion for the whole region. At the other side of the continent, Somalia has still not found peace to this day. Whatever the excesses committed by its political-military entrepreneurs, they have not yet obscured the memory of Siad Barre and of his responsibilities in setting off the conflict, or indeed those of the Western aid donors who supported him for so long because of the services he offered to the Free World.

Since the late 1980s, the debate on the state in Africa has at several points touched a wider current of thinking on the relationship between war and the formation of states, and on that between illicit economic activity and primitive capitalist accumulation. The first of these phenomena has certainly been of crucial importance in the history of Western Europe and Japan. The second is equally clear in the emergence of merchant capital in the sixteenth century, when the captains and merchants of the great sea-ports of northern Europe used the most villainous methods in their efforts to supplant those of Venice and Genoa. The Brentano, the famous Frankfurt merchant dynasty of the seventeenth century, took to money-laundering like Monsieur Jourdain did to speaking prose, long before the word had ever been uttered. These questions are all the more acute today, in part because of the opportunities offered to organized criminals by the globalization of markets, and partly because of the preponderance of military power over other social forces in most former colonies. 'In our own time, the analogy between war making and state making, on the one hand, and organized crime, on the other, is becoming tragically apt' (Tilly, 1985: 186).

In spite of these points of similarity, the problem of the criminalization of the states and economies of sub-Saharan Africa has its own historical specificity. It is not that the societies or the political systems of the sub-continent are more corrupt than others, as is so often believed. There is no reason to suppose that Japan, China, India, Russia, Turkey, Italy (or France for that matter) are any less tainted by this phenomenon. But, in Africa, the interaction between the practice of power, war, economic accumulation and illicit activities of various types forms a particular political trajectory which can be fully appreciated only if it is addressed in historical depth. One of the characteristics of this trajectory is the exploitation by dominant social groups, or by the dominant actors of the moment, of a whole series of rents generated by Africa's insertion in the international economy in a mode of dependence. Examples include the rents obtained from the control of exports of gold, ivory and slaves, or later from collaboration with colonial governments. Current examples include rents derived from diplomatic and military alliances, from the control of exports of agricultural goods and oil and of imports of all kinds, as well as from the management of external financing and aid. If one adds to this the observation that the dominated social groups also participate actively in the political economy of dependence, according to their scale and to the means at their disposal, it becomes clear that dependence is constructed and is maintained as much by African societies themselves as by the foreign actors who profit from these relationships. While the ideologies of democracy and humanitarianism which are so much in vogue at present may be used for both symbolic and material gratification, so the development of illicit activity south of the Sahara must be placed in the light of a particular history. It may continue in the same vein, or it may be capable of changing the practices enshrined or implied in this history.

It is high time, in fact, that the debate which began at the beginning of the 1990s should be placed on some form of scientific footing since it has been largely diverted along side-tracks which conform to moral considerations regarding governance, or concerning the appetites of presidents and entrepreneurs of violence. The question, from a scientific point of view, should be less one about the diversion of aid, even when it is offered for humanitarian purposes, or about corruption, even when it is political in nature, than it should concern the specific historical conditions which govern the processes of state formation and economic accumulation. It is in these terms that the rise of illicit activity south of the Sahara and its relations with ruling classes deserve to be analysed.

From the 1930s to the end of the 1970s, sub-Saharan Africa underwent an experience of economic growth based on the widespread, neo-mercantilist exploitation of primary resources, from which activity rents were extracted. This was spread across the sectors of agriculture, mining and oil. This economic model, constructed after the economic crash of 1929 and continued in the period of political liberalization after the Second World War, permitted the growth of a nationalist elite which, after independence, administered the system to its own benefit through the instruments of a state sector and parastatal companies. There were, naturally, ideological, political and social variants and performances which differed widely from one country to another. There are even cases of some states which do not conform to this general model.

But the enunciation of such a model has the advantage of underlining the specific characteristics of a historical sequence of events which, in most cases, represented a distinct rupture with the predatory economies of the nineteenth century and its prolongation into the colonial period, generally in the guise of concessionary companies and forced labour regimes. Today, this model seems to be ceding ground to a new mode of economic exploitation and insertion in the international system. If the structural and conjunctural causes of the crisis of the neo-mercantilist state are now well understood (the obsolescence of the structure of production and marketing, falls in the prices of commodities, the burden of internal and external debt, the loss of international competitiveness, the failure of structural adjustment), the precise character of the historical cycle which has enveloped Africa since the 1980s remains a matter for further investigation. One should not exclude the hypothesis of a revival of the predatory economy which predominated in the nineteenth century, provided that allowances are made for the radical changes in the nature and scale of this economy through the transformations which Africa and the world have undergone in the meantime. However, it may also be speculated that the participation of the sub-continent in illicit finance and trade may favour its growth and alter the manner of its insertion in the world economy, in the same way as seems to have occurred in Colombia, Thailand and southern China. As in South-East Asia, both scenarios could actually materialize at the same time in one region, with zones of conflict and war, susceptible to certain forms of criminal activity, complementing the economic activity of other areas which are apparently more respectable.

1

From Kleptocracy to the Felonious State?

JEAN-FRANÇOIS BAYART,
STEPHEN ELLIS &
BÉATRICE HIBOU

Africa south of the Sahara is often said to be in crisis. The naive enthusiasm which was such an outstanding characteristic of those who once made an ideology out of support for the Third World has given way to a gloomy prognosis which sometimes goes under the name of Afro-pessimism. In truth, there is little enough intellectual resistance to this Afro-pessimism other than a blind rush into the unknown – a *fuite en avant* – led by aid donors, who themselves have a vested interest in the matter. None of these intellectual conceits can be regarded as satisfactory. There can be no doubt of the fact that the sub-continent is undergoing serious difficulties of an economic and political nature. It is almost equally clear that, such a short time after Africa regained its independence, these difficulties are so acute as to put its place in the world in jeopardy. But any diagnosis as brief and summary as this risks underestimating the complexity of the crisis to which we refer, and of the responses which African societies are making to it. In the last thirty years Africa has undergone different crises: one caused by problems of bare subsistence, another being the threat of a Malthusian calamity, and a third concerning the uncertainty of its insertion in the international order. It is in particular the combination of the latter with the sluggishness of the present phase of the sub-continent's demographic transition which constitutes such a formidable problem today (Coussy and Vallin, 1996). One of the consequences of this particular conjuncture of factors is an erosion of the very foundations of political regimes, in much the same way as the transition from economies reliant on the slave trade to ones based on so-called 'legitimate' commerce in the nineteenth century was at the heart of a crisis of adaptation not just of systems of economic production, but of states themselves.

The fact that historians today are still locked in debate on the precise nature of the crisis of adaptation which occurred over a century ago is a powerful reminder of the need for prudence in any interpretation of Africa's current problems. No one can fail to be struck by the violence of the changes and the sheer scale of human suffering which have been generated by Africa's current crisis. None the less, several lines of research suggest that, even if the short-term outlook is dire, the long-term prospects are less sombre. The real indicators of economists and demographers suggest that the crisis of the sub-continent, multi-faceted though it may be, and the shock therapy which it has undergone have had less negative social consequences than might have been feared. This is in spite of the macro-economic ineffectiveness of structural adjustment programmes which has now been clearly demonstrated. Most notably, the societies which have been subject to such extreme destabilization are continually developing new strategies of an extraordinary diversity and inventiveness, which offers proof that Africa, so often said to be governed by age-old tradition, is in fact a place of unrivalled change and mobility. There is hardly a single sphere of life which has escaped transformations of great significance, of which the most obvious signs are the scale of migration, both voluntary and forced, and urbanization, or perhaps 'rurbanization'. It is thus a singular disservice to the richness and complexity of the reality to identify only five symptoms of change, as we now propose to do. These five, however, we believe to be particularly significant for the purpose of our analysis.

Five symptoms

1. The relegation of sub-Saharan Africa in diplomacy, economics and finance
Weakened by the economic and financial crisis which has affected it since the late 1970s, the sub-continent has been progressively devalued in the estimation of the great powers. The reasons for this include the end of the East–West rivalry of the Cold War and the beginnings of peace negotiations between Israel and its Arab neighbours – both conflicts from which African elites acquired a substantial political rent – and also the enhanced importance to the European Union, for various reasons, of the Maghreb, the Middle East and Eastern Europe. Contrary to what might have been expected, the Gulf War served to confirm the relegation, in geopolitical terms, of sub-Saharan Africa. The combination of this loss of diplomatic importance with an economic and financial crisis has resulted in a stark erosion of effective sovereignty in almost all the states of the region, which are submitted to an increasingly rigorous conditionality by aid donors in the course of structural

adjustment programmes. Oddly enough, the democratization process begun in 1989–91 under pressure from the urban population has actually increased the tendency towards the erosion of national sovereignty, since aid donors now attach conditions governing human rights to the loans and grants which they offer. But these conditions, however stringent in theory, are in fact applied with sufficient laxity as to have little effect on the substance of relations between the elites of the various *anciens régimes* and those people who are intent on pursuing a political revolution. They have, however, had the effect of obliging the main actors to change their system of legitimation.

Nevertheless it would be mistaken to think that sub-Saharan Africa's increased dependence is leading to its further marginalization in the world economy. Without doubt, the crisis of the 1980s was more acute in Africa than elsewhere. The economic performance of the sub-continent was particularly weak: African countries registered a loss of economic competitiveness in absolute terms, suffered a loss of international market-share in their traditional export products, and generally proved themselves incapable of acquiring a share of markets in new sectors. The marginalization of Africa in almost every legal market sector, with the exception of oil, is beyond question. Its share of world exports has declined, and in particular its share of world exports in manufactured goods is now so small as to be insignificant.

This under-performance is confirmed by figures for commodities as a percentage of total exports. The maintenance of a very high level of specialization in raw commodities (with a reduction of only 4 per cent between 1970 and 1990) is in marked contrast to the general figure for other developing countries, which saw the level of commodities as a proportion of total exports decline by 42 per cent over the same period.

In part, this is because there has been no significant development of the manufacturing sector. Again, this is a particular cause of concern in comparison with other developing countries. Figures from the 1986–94 period even suggest that the manufacturing sector has remained stagnant in the majority of African countries since independence, although aggregate statistics disguise some marked differences of performance.

Moreover, the loss of market share and the maintenance of a specialization in the export of raw materials have been aggravated by a sharp decline in recent years in the prices of the main export commodities. On the whole, this fall has not been compensated by any corresponding decline in the price of Africa's imports.

The decline of Africa's share in legal markets, however, has not led to its becoming disconnected from the world economy, or even to its being less integrated in this system. On the contrary, Africa remains highly integrated into the world economy and remains dependent upon it, not only by reason of its need to import but also because of its debt burden and the importance of the institutional and financial relations which it maintains with industrialized countries.

Even if we concede that official figures are frequent underestimates because of the scale of fraud, smuggling and under-invoicing, the important role played in African economies by the importation of goods from outside stems less from the monetary value of such goods than from the economic function of imports. In the first place, imports are overwhelmingly of consumer rather than capital goods. There is little hint of any process which leads to the adding of value, and no evidence at all that external dependency is decreasing. Secondly, imports have a definite lead-effect in regard to other sectors of the economy. Numerous studies of the informal economy have demonstrated the key role played in this sector by imported goods or inputs. Thirdly, state budgets rely heavily on receipts derived from import tariffs. Fourthly and last, imported goods are of crucial political and social importance. The management of imports, together with that of exports and of relations with the international financial institutions, gives access to one of the few available sites of accumulation of wealth and power. The formulation of external economic policy, the result of complex conflicts and compromises between various actors, is one of the most important instruments in economic and political life and has a determining effect on the process of social stratification, the formation of clientelist networks, and the penalization or co-optation of political opponents.

The importance of middle- and long-term foreign debt in economies which under-perform so spectacularly is another observation which cannot seriously be disputed. Debt service consumes a large proportion of Gross Domestic Product and, most particularly, of export earnings. The debt burden is in reality less than is implied by the ratio of debt service to export earnings because of the frequency with which debts are rescheduled or, in the case of the poorest countries, written off completely. It could even be argued that the debt burden is of little significance since the majority of African countries are incapable of servicing their debt and will never in fact repay it. Nevertheless, debt statistics remain a useful indicator of dependence in the sense that they provide a measure of the degree of influence exercised by the donor community, the importance of conditionality in the formulation of public policy, and the role of external finance, virtually the only source of investment.

2. The failure of the democratic transition promised by the liberalization of single-party governments at the end of the 1970s and by the mass political mobilization of 1989–92

With South Africa providing the only really important exception, the process of democratization has been captured, under the guise of competitive elections, by the authoritarian groups already in control of state power (notably in Côte d'Ivoire, Togo, Cameroon, Gabon and Kenya), or it has given rise to new regimes whose weakness offers little promise of future stability (Mali and Benin) or produced others which cannot easily be considered genuinely democratic (Central African Republic, Congo until 1997, Equatorial Guinea, Zambia, Chad), or else democracy has been snuffed out by the intervention of the armed forces (Nigeria, Niger, Burundi). Efforts to combine the requirements of a market economy with the demands of popular sovereignty have ended in failure. There can be no doubt that most of the hopes raised by the promise of democratization have now been dashed, in spite of the substantial achievements of the movements of the early 1990s in the fields of freedom of the press and freedom of association. After the tide of the reform movements had ebbed, the element of continuity between old and new regimes in both their social and political complexions became generally plain, even in cases where there had been a change of government, as in Mali or, more particularly, in Benin, Congo and Zambia. However, all these governments, even if they demonstrate a fundamental continuity in many ways, feel themselves obliged in the current system of international affairs to explore new methods of economic accumulation and political control. Hence, what we are actually witnessing is the reproduction of the authoritarian condition which was widespread in the postcolonial period; it has been modified by a certain degree of political and institutional reorganization but, more than anything else, it has adapted to the demands created by the crisis of the neo-mercantilist economies from which elites have for decades derived their incomes in the form of rents.

3. The continuation and spread of armed conflicts not only in areas where war has been endemic for decades, but also to parts of the subcontinent which have hitherto been spared
It would be an error to overlook the list of countries where a logic of violence has been replaced by a political process of negotiation and rebuilding. There are several such cases, some of them of considerable importance, such as South Africa, Uganda, Namibia, Mali, Eritrea, Ethiopia, Mozambique and, arguably, Angola. Nevertheless, it must be said that the list of war-torn countries south of the Sahara has tragically lengthened in recent years (Somalia, Guinea-Bissau, Rwanda, Burundi, Liberia, Sierra Leone, Senegal, the two republics of Congo) and may still see further additions if we take into account the fragility of certain states (Niger, Guinea, Cameroon, Central African Republic). Processes of transition from war to peace are by no means irreversible, even in Uganda, where an insurrectionary movement received clandestine help from the

former Zaïre and Sudan, or in Ethiopia, which is taking great risks by ethnicizing its institutions in conformity with its new constitution, or in South Africa, where the mediocre level of economic growth is hardly adequate for the country's social needs. It is notable that Africa's conflicts, even though they rarely take the form of wars directly between states, have an increasingly prominent regional dimension. (The Eritrean-Ethiopian conflict is an exception). Moreover, they may have grown in scale, at least if we are to judge by the number of deaths in the Great Lakes region, in Sudan, Liberia and Angola, by the development of urban battlefields in Mogadishu, Brazzaville, Bangui, Monrovia, Huambo, Kigali and Bujumbura, by the proliferation and commercialization of firearms spreading from the main centres of conflict, and by the effect which war is having on cultural or even metaphysical representations in the worst affected countries. Young Nuer recruits of the Sudan People's Liberation Army (SPLA) in South Sudan sing in Arabic (quoted in Hutchinson, 1996: 355):

> Even your mother, give her a bullet!
> Even your father, give him a bullet!
> Your gun is your food; your gun is your wife.

The indifference of the United States to the Liberian crisis in 1990 and the failure of US intervention in Somalia in 1993 have reduced the capacity of external powers to organize credible peacekeeping operations, as was tragically demonstrated by the impotence of the United Nations during the 1994 genocide in Rwanda or the fiasco of the projected humanitarian operation in Kivu in 1996.

4. The recomposition of the sub-continent around new foreign influences and axes of power
The main actors in the international system are inclined to disengage from a region whose geostrategic significance has declined and whose economic potential seems to have been placed on hold for an indefinite period. This withdrawal does not apply to all private operators, particularly in the mining and oil sectors and in the security business, but it does have a general discouraging effect on the most highly institutionalized forms of foreign presence. Both the US and the Member States of the European Union have been tempted to reduce their level of official development aid because of doubts about its effectiveness, the more so now that Russia is no longer a diplomatic player in Africa.

At the same time, third parties, particularly from the Middle East, South and East Asia and Eastern Europe and, to lesser extent, Latin America, are tending to fill this vacuum. Traders of the Lebanese, Indian, Pakistani and Chinese diasporas have returned in numbers after a period when policies of economic nationalism made life difficult for them, in the 1960s and 1970s. Various protagonists in the conflicts of the Near East, each trying to develop political bases to the opponent's rear, in Africa, intervene frequently via various economic or religious networks. Examples include Israel, whose African diplomacy has been largely privatized, and the oil monarchies of the Gulf. As for the countries of North Africa, including Egypt, they have never really filled the gap created to their south by decolonization but are increasingly active in the region. Thus, Africa is slowly reorienting itself – literally – by turning towards the East, to the detriment of European economic interests. This process is being aided by three main factors. The first of these is the financial difficulty faced by African states, which makes all the more tempting the promises of substantial 'parallel financing' offered by Middle Eastern or Chinese businessmen and the Taiwanese government. A second factor is the January 1994 devaluation of the CFA franc, which has reduced the competitiveness of West European businesses while enhancing the attractiveness of Asian products, encouraging business people south of the Sahara to buy directly by travelling either to East Asia or to the intermediary markets of the Gulf. A third consideration is the restrictive immigration policies of West European countries, and particularly of France, and the consequent difficulty for Africans to obtain entry visas. This has encouraged the reorientation of trade by obliging small traders in Africa to travel to Istanbul, the Gulf, or the Far East to make their purchases.

In addition, two poles of influence are developing within the sub-continent itself and could in time play a leading role in its recomposition. In West Africa, Nigeria with its 90 million or more inhabitants has shown itself capable of destabilizing the CFA franc zone by its own monetary and trade policies and of exercizing an increasingly blatant diplomatic and military influence in the region, for example in the form of its intervention in Liberia and Sierra Leone in the 1990s and its boundary disputes with Cameroon and Equatorial Guinea. In southern Africa, the government of South Africa enjoys the relative industrial and commercial dynamism which it inherited from its predecessor and can combine this with the political credit which it has derived from dismantling the system of apartheid. The gravity of its internal problems will no doubt prevent it from assuming the leadership of the region to the extent that it takes the place of the great powers, but there is no reason why this should prevent it from facilitating, in its own interest, the construction of 'development corridors' in its immediate vicinity and from enabling its own business community to capture a substantial part of the aid provided by Europe under the terms of the Lomé Convention. It may also be able to acquire new markets in Central and West Africa, and even to pursue its own political interest there through its secret services and its military apparatus. In this respect, South Africa's new governing party, the ANC, is following some of the trails developed by its predecessor without any great scruples (see Chapter 3).

5. The growing implication of African economic and political entrepreneurs (or European, Arab, Asian and Latin American operators who are based in Africa) in activities which may be considered illegal or criminal, according to Western criteria which have tended to be adopted by the international system as a whole

Corruption (or, more precisely, the combination of positions of public office with positions of accumulation) was always a feature of the mercantilist trade system which was at its zenith in Africa from 1930 to 1980. The phenomenon may be identified at the heart of colonial regimes and nationalist movements, as well as of postcolonial states which, in certain cases, gave rise to literal kleptocracies in the 1970s and 1980s, such as Zaïre, Nigeria, Sierra Leone, Liberia and Somalia. The straddling of multiple positions, such as of public office and of accumulation, was similarly characteristic of states in Western Europe at a certain period of their history, sometimes taking the form of a veritable economy of plunder of Mobutu-esque proportions, and it is also to be found in various political configurations in Asia, Latin America and the Middle East. We cannot over-emphasize the fact that the problem of what is commonly called 'corruption' is in no way unique to Africa.

Nevertheless, south of the Sahara, the radical form taken by practices of accumulation at or beyond the confines of the law, on the part of those who staff political institutions, suggests that a new form of *la politique du ventre*[1] may be emerging, in an international context which is new in at least two different respects. In the first place, international donors, in the name of good governance and the workings of the market, nowadays refuse to countenance practices which they previously tolerated in the name of the struggle against communism. In the second place, the international economy has undergone a number of profound changes, such as in the globalization of trade, the deregulation of markets and the growth of certain lucrative smuggling trades. This new environment provides significant new opportunities for such illegal activities.

Hence, the relationship between economic accumulation and tenure of political power in Africa now exists in new conditions. These have been created by the restoration of authoritarian regimes which

[1] Literally, 'the politics of the belly'. This is a Cameroonian expression which has numerous equivalents throughout sub-Saharan Africa. It denotes at the same time the accumulation of wealth through tenure of political power (implied in the proverb 'the goat grazes wherever it is tied'), the symbolic reference to family lineage and to witchcraft, and the physical corpulence which is felt to be appropriate in 'big men' or powerful women. A total social fact (to quote Marcel Mauss), *la politique du ventre* is a complex mode of government (see Bayart, 1993).

had lost their previous bases of legitimacy both in international circles and in the eyes of their domestic constituencies, through a process of economic and financial rot, by the erosion of state sovereignty and by the multiplication of armed conflicts covering entire regions. The relationship between accumulation and power is henceforth situated in a context of internationalization and of the growth of organized crime on a probably unprecedented scale. The world system is subject to a simultaneous process of globalization and loss of precise territorial definition, which may not lead to the eclipse of the state as an organ of power, but which is most surely leading to the development of transnational relations between societies. Criminal activities are greatly affected by this evolution, and quite often they thrive in this environment. Criminal operators, who can on occasion be formidably well organized at a national level and in some cases exercise clear influence at the heart of the state, or even use the state as their main power-base, as in Italy, Colombia, Japan, China, India and Russia, are capable of co-operation with one another and even on occasion of launching true joint ventures. At the same time, criminal activity often serves as a vehicle for both cultural representations and goods of foreign origin, and in this respect plays a full role in the process of globalization. It is interesting to note in passing that criminals are very often portrayed as heroes in feature films and television programmes.

Although organized crime operating on a worldwide scale is nowadays the subject of considerable attention, especially in its relation to political power, it is debatable whether its alleged growth is not an optical illusion caused by the new-found zeal of magistrates and journalists. In any event, the variety of situations subsumed under the fashionable heading of 'mafias' is diverse in the extreme. Whatever the exact truth of this matter, the fact is that the global context in which major criminal organizations operate gives them a certain functional coherence, and even a political and cultural one, which may also prove to be the case in sub-Saharan Africa in conformity with the trend towards what might be called 'glocalization'.

Evidence for such a development might be adduced from Africa's growing role in the carriage of narcotics. Sub-Saharan Africa has become a staging-post of world importance for heroin en route from Asia's Golden Triangle to the markets of North America and, to a lesser but rapidly growing extent, for cocaine imported from Latin America and awaiting re-export to Western Europe. Narcotics transported to the Persian Gulf are also reported to transit via Africa, although on a scale which is rather more difficult to evaluate. Nigeria is the country most directly implicated in the narcotics trade as a whole, and is the country south of the Sahara regarded by American law enforcement agencies with the most concern. The attention which law enforcement officers now attach to Nigeria and the suspension of direct flights between Lagos and the United States have caused drug smugglers to develop new trade routes, notably through Togo, Côte d'Ivoire, Cape Verde, Sierra Leone, Liberia, Mauritania, Zimbabwe, South Africa and, especially, Ghana and Senegal. The prominent role now played by Nigeria in this trade should not obscure the fact that other countries, such as Ethiopia and Kenya, also have well-established positions in the same commerce. It would certainly be prudent not to develop too rigid an analysis of this trade since drug routes change constantly, not least as smugglers respond to new patterns of surveillance by customs officials and airport security officers. Trade routes tend to follow new 'short cuts' and to 'splinter' easily, in the words of the Paris-based Observatoire géopolitique des drogues (1995: 6–14). These tendencies have not prevented African drug networks from acquiring international importance. Couriers frequently change nationality, thanks to the ease with which legal procedures can be bypassed and false passports or other documents obtained. Major drug syndicates are now solidly implanted in the main areas of production (especially South-East Asia), the main transit hubs (for example, Istanbul, southern Italy and the Iberian peninsula), and the main consumer countries (Western Europe and the US). Members of African drug syndicates are reported to have established themselves in Bolivia, Russia, Central Europe, and even in China. They are increasingly equipped to avoid Africa altogether in their efforts to arrange a constant supply of narcotics.

The most prominent drug networks in the continent are without doubt Nigerian, and especially Ibo. These are said to control up to 70 or 80 per cent of Burmese heroin reaching the American market and up to 35 or 40 per cent of heroin of all origin going to the United States. Among the features which have led to the success of the Nigerian syndicates are well-developed techniques for hiding illicit goods, the large-scale recruitment of individual 'mules' or couriers, and the ethnic and linguistic homogeneity of the leading syndicates, which makes them more or less impenetrable by outsiders. No doubt some elements of this description must be regarded with caution, as US drug enforcement agencies occasionally modify the data which they publish, for operational or political reasons. The Clinton Administration, for example, has on occasion refused to certify Iran as a non-offender although, on the admission of State Department staff themselves, it has no hard evidence of the implication of the Islamic Republic in narcotics trafficking. For the same reason, it would be wise to regard with caution recent accusations launched against the government of Sudan. There can be no serious doubt, however, that Nigerian drug syndicates, beginning with networks of individual couriers hiring out their services to carry up to two kilograms of heroin hidden inside their bodies (with a street value of up to US$2 million in New York), have proceeded to upgrade the level at which they are inserted into the international division of labour in the narcotics trade since they were able to establish their independence in the mid-1980s. It appears that, since then, Nigerian gangs have established networks which are able to operate at both ends of the chain which links the transport of heroin between the Golden Triangle and the markets of North America, enabling them to deal directly with the major drug organizations of South-East Asia, and at the same time to provide the European market with a growing supply of Latin American cocaine. They are able to employ a growing number of white couriers, notably US and South African nationals, so as to evade detection at immigration controls in the major airports of the West. They also make considerable use of commercial sea, road and air-freight routes to transport larger quantities of merchandise in relative security.

It is difficult to establish the nature of the relationship, if any, between the major Nigerian syndicates and other African networks, such as the Ghanaian, Senegalese, Zaïrean and Tanzanian smugglers who are increasingly active in Western Europe and South Africa. To judge from the rise of these new groups, the role of the Lebanese diaspora in the African drug trade, so often regarded as being a leading one, is perhaps less important than has often been supposed. It certainly seems less salient than that of Nigeria, in spite of the importance of certain Lebanese families close to the Nigerian military government, while, in the case of Zaïre, Lebanese implication in the drug trade was certainly exaggerated by sources hostile to the government of President Mobutu.

The rise in importance of African drug networks appears all the more formidable since they are able to make use, for their own organizational ends, of the cultural resources of highly flexible, acephalous societies with well-established merchant traditions. Here, the case of the Ibo of eastern Nigeria is instructive in more than one respect. The comparative advantage of African drug traffickers, in a market of literally cut-throat competitiveness, stems from their membership of segmentary, decentralized and flexible communities, endowed with a high reputation for commercial expertise developed over generations. The distinction between these and the structures of Latin American and Italian mafias, which are hierarchical and subject to the control of established bosses or *capos,* is worthy of note.

The example of Colombia provides an illustration of how the revolution in the drug trade has been aided by factors which are present in abundance south of the Sahara. These include a culture which values individual effort and success, in which the end is held to justify the means (in particular through recourse to cunning or deception), a conception of social ascent which draws upon the repertoire of magical control, well-adapted to the sudden enrichment which is typical of success in the drug trade, the artisanal mining of precious stones which could play the same role in Africa as the emerald trade played in Colombia in paving the way for the establishment of drug trafficking networks, and the widespread practice of smuggling and fraud, which are also classic historical matrices of successful drug trafficking environments. In addition, African drug syndicates are able to profit from a growing demand within the continent itself: the consumption of amphetamines, heroin and cocaine is increasing at an alarming rate, notably in West Africa. South Africa, traditionally a market for Indian-produced mandrax imported via Mozambique, Namibia and, most particularly, Zimbabwe and Zambia, is considered by specialists to have great potential as a market for heroin and cocaine (see Chapter 3).

Sub-Saharan Africa seems less well-placed to develop a drug processing industry, although it is reasonable to speculate on the possible future role of the small-scale chemical, plastics and cosmetics industries controlled by Lebanese, Chinese and African entrepreneurs, such as in Nigeria and Côte d'Ivoire.

The actual cultivation of narcotic plants on a large scale, other than the traditional marijuana, is by no means a foregone conclusion, even if experiments with new strains of cannabis and with opium poppies have been recorded in many places and even though certain areas offer excellent agricultural and climatic conditions for the eventual development of coca cultivation. One reason for this is that the prices paid to producers internationally are too low to provide real incentives to enter production and Africa has no obvious comparative advantage which would enable it to compete in production with the Golden Triangle, the Golden Crescent, or the republics of Central Asia and Latin America. The service activities linked to the drug trade, especially transport, are infinitely more lucrative than production itself, as Colombian drug entrepreneurs realized at an early stage, and in any case the economic traditions of most parts of Africa are best adapted to the service function. It is none the less probable that drug production intended for the local consumer market, what one might call subsistence drug cultivation, will gain ground as the size of Africa's urban population increases, and that this will become a mainstay of regional trade networks, as is already the case with the marketing of the legally permitted stimulant *khat* in the Horn of Africa. Such a development appears all the more likely in view of the fact that military activity, which, we have noted, is in rapid expansion, is generally associated in Africa with the use of stimulants. This was already noted in the Congolese rebellions of 1964–5 and in the Biafran war. Today, combatants in the various conflicts in Liberia,

Sierra Leone and Somalia smoke, swallow and chew with abandon, and the regular soldiers of ECOMOG (the peacekeeping force established in 1990 at the behest of Nigeria by the Economic Community of West African States to supervise and enforce a ceasefire in the Liberian civil war) are also no strangers to the use of drugs. The militiamen who carried out the genocide of Tutsi in Rwanda in 1994 frequently operated under the influence of drugs, as do the gangs of killers operating in Burundi today.

The relativity of processes of criminalization

While the process of restoring authoritarian rule and the extension of armed conflicts south of the Sahara have been the subject of fairly precise analysis, the criminalization of economies and of states in Africa, the subject of the current study, has inspired little more than embarrassed silence and sensational newspaper reports. It deserves deeper consideration.

The very definition of what is and what is not criminal is, to be sure, eminently relative and varies over time even within a given society. In the French legal lexicon, the term 'to criminalize' has a number of precise technical meanings, such as in regard to a matter referred to a criminal court by an appropriate civil organ. A crime is not in itself deemed to have any immediate substance, and French jurists, for example, distinguish between 'primary criminalization', which is pronounced by an investigating body, and 'secondary criminalization', which occurs when a matter is effectively submitted to a due process of law. The matter which is the object of the secondary criminalization is introduced into the judicial system by an incrimination, that is, a formal decision to prosecute the person or persons alleged to have committed a crime. This process leads to a submission of the case to the judgement of a criminal court, which has the power to impose a sentence. The court judgement has both a legal meaning and a wider moral one, cultural notions *par excellence*. The notions of criminalization and incrimination, however, are not only the constructions of a specific cultural system which displays a certain relativity while pretending to universal application. Even in quite a short period of time, the criteria of primary criminalization may vary markedly within a single cultural system, and this gives rise to periodic debates such as that between proponents and opponents of the decriminalization of 'soft' drugs in the European Union or that in ecological circles, in the US and various parts of Northern Europe, which arises from a quasi-religious conception of the protection of nature. Africa has witnessed particularly rapid changes in the normative conception of what is and is not criminal. To cite only two examples, the United Kingdom and the US in 1807 and 1808 declared the continent's main export – slaves – to be illegal, while residents of South Africa were for some decades forbidden by law to engage in inter-racial sexual relations.

These distinctions are of direct practical importance. In the first place, they may clear the way for a rational consideration of certain policies of prohibition or restriction applied by industrialized countries, most notably in the fields of the narcotics trade, immigration and the protection of the environment, even though there are limits to any utilitarian conception of markets and their imperfections. A considerable number of commentators see in the decriminalization or legalization of drugs the only effective means of devaluing the rents to be derived from the criminal status of the trade in, and consumption of, those substances which are defined as narcotic. Advocates of legalization suggest dissociating the very real problem which such products pose to public health from the economic aspects of their commercialization. By the same token, in sub-Saharan Africa, the criminal offence of poaching protected species of wildlife and the militarization of hunting activities which is induced by this legal qualification, as well as the criminal violence on the part of both poachers and game wardens which is a result, are all consequences of the designation of game reserves and protected species, restrictions on hunting and the ideology of environmentalism which justifies the death of human beings in the name of protecting endangered species.

Such perverse or unintended consequences of policies of restriction or prohibition tend to be cumulative in their effect. Hence, there are reports that gangs and networks specialized in trading in drugs are increasingly using their expertise and resources to service the market in illegal migrant workers in Western Europe, where strict immigration policies have created lucrative market opportunities for smugglers and, by the same token, drug networks lend themselves easily to trade in, for example, endangered species of wildlife.

It should be noted at this juncture that some social actors in Africa do not necessarily share the opinions of their foreign counterparts in matters of this sort and see nothing immoral in participating in certain types of activity which are considered criminal in the West. This seems to be the case with drug trafficking, which certain traders in Nigeria do by stealth only as a result of pressure from abroad but which some people seek to justify, sometimes in public, by reference to various historical precedents (beginning, inevitably, with that of the slave trade). A rather better example is that of the financial frauds known in Nigeria as '419' (see Chapter 4). To a considerable degree, such attitudes may be explained by a particularly gross cynicism, given that, in some of the countries concerned, people in positions of public authority have set a precedent in diverting public resources for their private benefit or in dumping toxic waste in return for personal reward, showing an impressive contempt for the health of their fellow-citizens. We would, however, be deceiving ourselves if we were to go no further than this in analysing the matter. The rise in Africa of activities officially classed as criminal is aided by the existence of moral and political codes of behaviour, especially those of ethnicity, kinship and even religion, and of cultural representations, notably of the invisible, of trickery as a social value, of certain prestigious styles of life, even of an aesthetic,[2] whose capacity to legitimize certain types of behaviour is considerable (see Chapter 2). In more general terms, some fundamental categories of modern economics are not viewed in the same manner by Western investors, traders and aid donors on the one hand, and their African partners on the other.

These ambiguities lie at the heart of certain recurrent social phenomena to be found in contemporary Africa, including the instances of wholesale looting of cities, banditry, prostitution and fraud. Thus, for the purposes of our analysis, we require a precise and usable definition of what exactly constitutes crime and criminality, even at the risk of creating a rather narrow and arbitrary definition. For present purposes, and in the perspective of the study of international relations, we shall regard as criminal those political, social and economic practices which are the object of a 'primary criminalization' either by the laws and other texts of the states which are under discussion or, more particularly, in international law, or according to international organizations or acknowledged guardians of international morality, and especially the financial and economic morality which accompanies the current trend towards the globalization of the economy.

A partial list of criminal practices according to such criteria would include trades in human beings, drugs, nuclear material and works of art; piracy and banditry; certain threats to the environment such as the trades in ivory and endangered species of wild animals and the unregulated dumping of toxic waste; various economic or financial practices or malpractices which constitute forms of fraud or embezzlement (the pilfering of foreign aid, the illegal export of capital or natural resources, the large-scale counterfeiting of patented products, systematic tax evasion, the laundering of money from illegal transactions), or practices which are illegal in virtually every national legislation, such as the counterfeiting of banknotes; and the illegitimate use of the state's coercive resources or of resources of violent coercion which are private and, hence, illegitimate.

---

[2] Modern criminologists have drawn attention to 'cultural styles' and aesthetics which assist in the constitution of criminality. See Ferrell and Sanders (1995).

This last category is in fact inadequate as a description of the major political shift which, we suggest, is occurring in sub-Saharan Africa. The illegitimate use of violence now takes place on a massive scale, including at the behest of those who actually hold formal political and public office as they undertake wars or as they struggle to restore authoritarian regimes which are under threat, but also in the form of uncontrolled delinquency in general. In essence, consideration of such illegitimate violence may be situated within the more familiar debates on human rights, public liberties and the centralization of the state. As for the notion of economic delinquency, this covers a gamut of practices of corruption and plunder which can attain spectacular proportions in conditions where authoritarian regimes are struggling to reassert themselves (Cameroon, Zaïre, Kenya) or in time of war (systematic looting of industrial infrastructure by the Rwandan Armed Forces in Rwanda during their retreat in 1994, notably at Cyangugu, or by the Nigerian army in Liberia, notably at Buchanan, in the course of service with ECOMOG). Plunder of this sort was already characteristic of authoritarian, neo-mercantilist regimes in the past.

Both the illegitimate use of violence and economic delinquency are best understood in relation to political strategies, wider social and economic changes and international developments which confer on them a new meaning and which may be seen as evidence of profound changes in the sub-continent. In the present study we shall dwell only on those criminal practices which are collective or highly organized and which exhibit a marked or even organic relationship with tenure of political power or the institutions of the state. It is in this sense that we shall leave to one side the strictly juridical definition of criminalization and shall define it, at the risk of using a somewhat inelegant neologism, as the invasion of the political arena by such practices. *The criminalization of politics and of the state may be regarded as the routinization, at the very heart of political and governmental institutions and circuits, of practices whose criminal nature is patent, whether as defined by the law of the country in question, or as defined by the norms of international law and international organizations or as so viewed by the international community, and most particularly that constituted by aid donors.*

Defined thus, criminalization can hardly be the subject of any exact quantification. By definition, statistics regarding smuggling and other criminal activities are no more than estimates or rough approximations. In the present context, a number of other difficulties add to this lack of precision to make a quantitative analysis more difficult still. First, the informal element in African economies is of crucial importance, although it is not possible to measure the size of the informal economy exactly, not least because it exists in constant symbiosis with the formal economy (Hibou, 1996). It is nowadays recognized that the major aggregate indicators, such as figures of Gross Domestic Product, levels of production and economic activity, sectoral growth rates, statistics of purchasing power and so forth, do not reflect the reality of the economies which they purport to represent and cannot be considered as wholly viable. In these circumstances it becomes all the more difficult to estimate, among the mass of informal economic activities, the proportion of those whose criminal character is paramount.

Secondly, the data which are compiled in balance-of-payments statistics should be treated with caution. In fact, among all the various classifications in this category only the figures for aid provided by the main donors can be taken as definite guides to reality. Imports and exports are both subject to substantial under- and over-invoicing. Fraud and smuggling take place on a massive scale. It is impossible to separate simple fraud from more sophisticated illicit operations. Debt statistics are often the result of rough estimates and are to be treated with caution on these grounds alone. The capital movements which may be deduced from these figures are thus unreliable in the extreme. Among the most trustworthy statistics are those published by the Bank for International Settlements, but it remains impossible to distinguish capital flows resulting from specific criminal activities, such as those derived from the laundering of drug money, from those arising from more 'classical' forms of illegal activity such as flight capital or tax evasion, or even from legal flows such as the remittance of profits earned abroad and settlement of bills for imported goods.

Thirdly, quantitative data on criminal activity, even more than other statistics, are largely gathered according to political criteria and pressures and are thus, more than most others, to be handled with care. In particular, figures on the drug trade are to be regarded as particularly sensitive when the extent to which they may have a bearing on the foreign policies of the main aid-giving nations is appreciated. It is thus quite likely that official US sources over-estimate the Nigerian role in the international heroin trade and that the French authorities under-estimate that of the franc zone in money-laundering activities.

Fourthly and lastly, the information which is produced by public bodies in donor countries and by multilateral institutions is particularly inaccessible, no doubt as a consequence of the sensitivity of the subject. In Africa itself, the organizations charged with the task of data collection often lack experience, use different collection methods and are embarrassed by the role played by a section of the national elites in the very activities which they are supposed to monitor.

In spite of these reservations, the obstacles to a quantitative approach to an analysis of the impact of criminal activities on African economies are not of such a nature as to prevent any further inquiry.

In effect, one may wonder whether the phenomenon which we describe as criminalization is not best considered as a qualitative change which is transforming the overall manner in which whole societies and the international system of diplomacy and commerce are organized, by changing the balance of forces between the fundamental determinants of any political order: power, accumulation, and the exercise of violence.

Crime and politics south of the Sahara

If it is approached in the way we have suggested above, the problem of the criminalization of the state in sub-Saharan Africa appears to be one of great contemporary relevance, but also of great diversity. On the one hand, authoritarian regimes continue to make use of tried and tested practices, sometimes in a form more systematic than in the past. This is the case notably when such regimes are associated with 'strategies of tension' manipulated or controlled by tyrants seeking to restore their fortunes (Zaïre, Cameroon, Kenya, Togo), or sometimes in diluted form, such as in Côte d'Ivoire, in the twilight years of Félix Houphouët-Boigny, during the premiership of Alassane Ouattara.

On the other hand, it is notable that new regimes, even when they have been democratically elected, and new forms of political mobilization, such as militias and armed groups, constitute vectors of criminalization. In Zaïre, the main opposition party, the Union pour la démocratie et le progrès social (UDPS), had no hesitation in helping itself to a share of the available booty in the diamond trade. In Zambia, several leading members of the governing party have been implicated in drug scandals. In Madagascar, Congo and the Central African Republic, presidents newly elected by universal suffrage have sought 'parallel financing' from organizations which are clearly fronts for money-laundering or for fraud on the grand scale. The implication of military or paramilitary organizations in the wholesale looting of cities, in the theft of humanitarian aid and in trafficking in drugs, diamonds or other natural resources has been apparent in Liberia, Sierra Leone, Somalia, Burundi, Rwanda. It has been the pattern for a longer period in Chad, Angola, and Mozambique, to the point where several conflicts south of the Sahara can be better understood as stemming from the economic logic of predation rather than of any political, ethnic or regional calculus.

Several branches of criminal activity, without being entirely new, are clearly assuming a greater importance. Apart from drug trafficking and the laundering of the profits of criminal activity, which we shall study in more detail in Chapter 4, the illegal export of diamonds, gold, precious or at least valuable minerals, agricultural products, works of art and game meat seems to be increasing at an impressive speed, particularly, but certainly not exclusively, in former Zaïre, even though other illegal exports may be in decline, such as in ivory, because of the reduction in demand caused by the banning of the international ivory trade in 1989. The sovereign right to mint currency has been flouted in several countries by importing or printing banknotes without any form of supervision by the central bank or the ministry of finance, and in such a manner that colossal sums have been diverted for private use, generally at the instigation of politically influential figures, such as in Zaïre and Kenya. Certain merchant networks which are relatively independent of political power, such as among the Ibo of Nigeria, are reported to have imported entire containers of counterfeit banknotes from Korea and Taiwan. Last but not least, the question arises whether sub-Saharan Africa is not witnessing a revival of the traffic in human beings. In several countries, members of the political elite are owners of night clubs which are well known as centres of prostitution, and are even suspected of involvement in networks of organized prostitution in Europe. Perhaps more importantly, some armed groups have moved on from enlisting young people as soldiers by force, as both UNITA and the MPLA have done in Angola and RENAMO has done in Mozambique, to forcing people into slavery for purposes of economic production, as has happened in Sierra Leone and especially in Liberia, or exporting captives for sale, for example from southern Sudan and, possibly, the east of Chad and the Central African Republic.

A first impression would suggest that the process of criminalization as we have defined it has become the dominant trait of a sub-continent in which the state has literally imploded under the combined effects of economic crisis, neo-liberal programmes of structural adjustment and the loss of legitimacy of political institutions. The simple capacity to administer of even the best established regimes is diminishing, for example in Cameroon, Côte d'Ivoire and Senegal. It is further eroded by the emigration of the best trained people and by privatization schemes which concern not just the public sector of the economy but also the main institutions of national sovereignty, such as the customs service and the organs of public security and national defence. In large swathes of sub-Saharan Africa, the capacity to execute any form of policy has quite simply evaporated and its place has been taken, at least to some extent, by churches and religious sodalities, a burgeoning informal economy, and military organizations and militias or other armed movements which are sometimes home-grown, sometimes foreign. It is by no means evident that the chancelleries of the donor governments fully understand that the Africa with which they maintain relations is often no more than a decor of *trompe-l'oeil* and that whole regions have now become virtually independent, probably for the fore-seeable future, of all central control and even of those economic and political structures which are most familiar to Western analysts. Discourses concerning 'good governance', 'civil society' and the virtues of 'the other path' represented by the informal economy, intended by donors as therapeutic remedies, are more surreal than real when considered in relation to what is happening in Liberia, Sierra Leone, Chad and the Central African Republic, where the only effective law is frequently that of the various armed bands whose political and moral codes, informal though they be, are certainly not those of the World Bank.[3] The same observation can be made of a country like Senegal whose capital, Dakar, appears ever more as the mere shadow, the this-worldly mirror of Touba, holy city of the Mouride brotherhood and a national capital of fraud and smuggling. There are entire states which for many years already have specialized in the import and re-export of more or less licit products coming from neighbouring countries. The description of them by economists as 'entrepôt states' is merely a euphemism: they are in fact smuggling states or states which indulge in fraud on the grand scale – Gambia, Togo, Benin, Equatorial Guinea, Burundi, Somalia – whose influence on neighbouring countries we underestimate at our peril.

It requires considerable optimism and imagination to believe that the governments which currently exist, and their bureaucracies, have the means necessary to implement the deep structural reforms which are nowadays required of them, for example in regard to fiscal policy, even supposing that they have the political will to do so. But the survival of the franc zone, the success of structural adjustment programmes and of regional economic integration, the pillars on which the aid donors base their policies, all suppose the success of prior reforms.

The division of African social systems into a legal edifice which is the partner of multilateral institutions and Western governments, and the real fabric of society, which is something different, is itself an indicator of the process of criminalization. Several of the African governments which have gone the furthest in this process of deregulation are characterized by the existence of a hidden and collective structure of power which surrounds, and even controls, the official tenants of state power. Hidden power-brokers of this sort are able to use to their advantage the privatization of legitimate means of coercion, and even to use with impunity private and illegitimate organs of coercion in the form

---

[3] In April 1995, an official of the World Bank with responsibility for Central Africa informed us in an interview, apparently in all seriousness, of his satisfaction with the progress of structural adjustment in Chad since the formal economy had been destroyed by war and conditions were thus ripe for the development of a free market economy.

of paramilitary organizations or even criminal gangs. They exploit for their own profit public enterprises and financial institutions or regulatory bodies such as marketing boards, but they also abuse the liberalization of economic institutions by means including privatization, fraud and smuggling through the use of intermediaries, front-men and personalized networks. In the most extreme cases these hidden structures of power function as effective boards of directors chaired by the official head of state, who in some cases may dispose of no more than a delegated authority. Thus, the real power of the head of state may vary according to such factors as his degree of autonomy, the relative weight of individual personalities within the board of directors, and those elements which a president is able to manipulate within the formal institutions of state, in regard to economic accumulation, in international or regional affairs, and in regard to the invisible powers of the spiritual world. Political life in Africa consists first and foremost of the management of factional intrigues for personal interest. It is for this reason that it often displays a wilfully enigmatic or even irrational-seeming attitude to the major political questions identified by aid donors. The political life of the continent is less likely to follow a linear path of reform and structural adjustment than to represent simply the outcome of conflicts of interest between dominant factions. The resources on which such a political life draws are diverse in the extreme. They include the resources of power in the classic sense, but also economic and financial resources which become available in the context of the widespread practice of looting and the privatization of the state, the diplomatic and military resources which emanate from the spread of armed conflicts to assume a level of regional importance, and the resources of the spiritual world represented by the sub-continental scope of operation of the leading marabouts and practitioners in spiritual matters.

The division of the structure of power into a real entity and a legal fiction has been documented with some precision in the case of Sierra Leone during the presidencies of Siaka Stevens and Joseph Momoh by William Reno (1995), who refers to it as a 'shadow state', and in regard to Rwanda between 1990 and 1994, where the *akazu*, the house of the presidential family, was able to demonstrate in rivers of blood the reality of its grasp of power. Comparable phenomena may be identified in Cameroon, where the 'Beti lobby' is ubiquitous, in Chad, where the Presidential Guard and its Zaghawa associates are actively engaged in operations best described as predation, and in the Central African Republic, where the Yakoma clan had such great influence on President Kolingba and where people of the ilk of Jean-Jacques Demafouth enjoy influence with President Patassé. In Congo, great power was wielded by the informal lobby surrounding President

Lissouba known as the Nibolek, especially in the persons of Claudine Munari, chief of staff in the president's office, Martin Mberi, minister of state and head of the 'Presidential Reserve', the government's praetorian guard, and Auguste Ngembo, head of the private militia known as 'the Zulus'. In Kenya, an example is provided by the power of the Kalenjin coterie and, most prominent among it, of Nicholas Biwott. One may equally wonder whether Marshal Mobutu, whose authority for so many years was uncontested, was not for a substantial period the hostage of what we have called a 'board of directors', consisting in his case of the Equatorian clique from his home province, and the military barons of the government.

Clandestine power structures of this sort have, since 1991, made decisive contributions to various processes in the restoration of authoritarian regimes which are under threat by encouraging and financing 'strategies of tension', as they are called in Italy. Operation Mygale in Cameroon, the radical politics of 'Hutu power' which resulted in the Rwandan genocide, the crucial interventions of the Togolese army in the attempted democratization of 1991 or the campaigns of ethnic cleansing carried out in Kenya's Rift Valley, all constitute clear examples of this process.

In cases of this sort, people who are relatively little known, sometimes with no official title or position whatsoever, are able to exercise political influence and occupy key economic posts which bear no relation to their degree of institutional 'visibility', in many instances because of the occult spiritual powers which they claim and with which they are credited, but also by having recourse to a privatized coercive capacity in the form of gangs or militias who attack, rob, rape and murder opponents or competitors, sometimes including fellow members of the informal national board of directors. The murders, some of a highly ritualized nature, of a dozen clerics in Cameroon or of Robert Ouko, the Minister of Foreign Affairs, in Kenya, for example, appear to have been motivated by the need to eliminate witnesses in possession of compromising information, potential rivals, or former colleagues who had changed their ways and were threatening to testify in public as to their previous activities. Such figures of the shadows, often cultivated by Western exporters, investors, diplomats, security officials and intelligence officers on account of the services they can render or their role as gate-keepers to the inner state, nowadays seem increasingly inclined not merely to interfere in affairs of national economic importance, but actually to participate directly in economic activities considered by the international community to be criminal in nature.

Recent experience, for example in Cameroon, Chad, the Central African Republic, Congo, former Zaïre and Kenya, has illustrated the extent to which aid donors are impotent when faced with such shadow structures of power and accumulation. Donor governments have shown themselves unable or unwilling to impose any serious conditionality in regard to either economic and financial matters or political affairs. In economic and financial matters especially, the existence of shadow structures of power is made manifest by the weakness of the real powers of the official institutional partner of the donors, that is to say, the national ministry of the economy or finance. A ministry of finance is in fact undermined, on the one hand, by the formal supervisory role played by the International Monetary Fund, the World Bank and the aid donors, and, on the other hand, by the informal and hidden sway of unofficial power-brokers who work in the murky demimonde of the second economy.

In political matters, ministers of foreign affairs have never been the real tenants of diplomatic power in Africa, and those among them who forget the absolute pre-eminence of heads of state and their personal entourages in this respect often learn or re-learn this fact the hard way. By personalizing its Africa policy, often in a most extreme form, France has made its own contribution to an informalization of the foreign relations of a number of sub-Saharan countries, as have some major foreign companies, especially mining and oil companies, which, in a similar way, often prefer to deal directly with the head of state rather than with the relevant minister or official.

Beyond the fact that the members of unofficial 'boards of directors' are among the leading operators and beneficiaries of the economy of plunder, fraud and smuggling which we shall discuss further in due course, Africa is today linked to the rest of the world by a complex web of informal political, commercial and financial relations which generally have a strong ethnic, corporatist or communal element. Even when it was discredited in the eyes of the international community, Zaïre, for example, continued to trade intensively with the rest of the world by means of its many privately owned air charter companies and lorry fleets. Nande traders from Kivu work in markets in Dubai and Hong Kong via Sudan and the ports of the Indian Ocean or directly by air freight, while other networks export the minerals of Shaba or the diamonds of Kasai via South Africa, Matadi or Kinshasa and import via overland road haulage from Nigeria (see Figure 1.2). The Somali ethnic diaspora, in spite of conditions in the home country, still occupies an important position in transport routes throughout East Africa and Somali traders shuttle between this area and the Gulf countries, Italy and North America, while the Senegalese Mouride religious brotherhood has been closely associated with successful trading enterprises around the Mediterranean rim and on the east coast of the United States where, together with South Korean

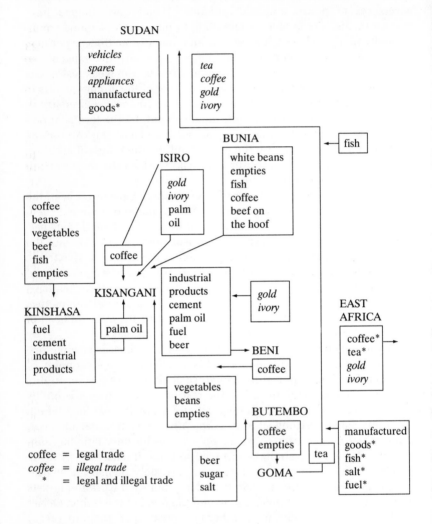

Figure 1.1 Flow chart of commodities traded in north-east Zaïre
Source: Janet MacGaffey, *Entrepreneurs and Parasites,* Cambridge University Press, Cambridge, 1987

traders, Mouride entrepreneurs have taken a substantial share of the retail distribution of electrical goods.

The social categories which are involved in conflicts and economic processes which may appear to the outside observer as being parochial in the extreme are themselves in contact with the world system or systems and are usually aware of this fact. Hence, not only do young fighters in Sierra Leone and Liberia dig diamonds which will be sold in London or Antwerp, sometimes passing through the hands of De Beers, but in some cases they have adopted as one of their cultural heroes Rambo, whose exploits they watch on videos in their camps. Not all of these informal commercial networks are necessarily associated with illicit activity other than smuggling or fraud, but the evidence strongly suggests that they are likely to participate in the criminalization of African states in future if this process indeed progresses as it seems set fair to do.

Even if it is impossible to provide a reasonably sophisticated statistical evaluation of the degree to which states are themselves becoming agents of criminal activity, for the reasons mentioned above, it is none the less necessary to proceed beyond the accumulation of hard evidence or of individual anecdotes to try and state the nature and scale of the phenomenon succinctly. Our hypothesis, that politics in Africa is becoming markedly interconnected with crime, can be further tested only if we are able to identify relatively precise criteria which distinguish the phenomenon which we call criminalization from other more classic forms of corruption, predation or kleptocracy. It is the cumulative weight of these criteria, or at least of a critical number of them, which will allow the observer to identify a definite rupture with earlier forms of the mode of governance which we have referred to as *la politique du ventre*.

We shall propose *six indicators of the criminalization of politics:*

1. the use for private purposes of the legitimate organs of state violence by those in authority, and the function of such violence as an instrument in the service of their strategies of accumulation of wealth;
2. the existence of a hidden, collective structure of power which surrounds and even controls the official occupant of the most senior political office, and which benefits from the privatization of the legitimate means of coercion, or is able with impunity to have recourse to a private and illegitimate apparatus of violence, notably in the form of organized gangs;
3. the participation by this collective and semi-clandestine power structure in economic activities considered to be criminal in international law, or which are so classified by international

organizations or in terms of moral codes which enjoy wide international currency;

4. the insertion of such economic activities in international networks of crime;
5. an osmosis between a historically constituted culture which is specific to the conduct of such activities in any given society and the transnational cultural repertoires which serve as vehicles for processes of globalization;
6. the macroeconomic and macropolitical importance, as distinct from the occasional or marginal role, of such practices on the part of power-holders and of these activities of accumulation in the overall architecture of a given society.

By following this line of reasoning we arrive at a somewhat paradoxical observation. For, on the one hand, few of the countries south of the Sahara fulfil a sufficient number of our six criteria to qualify for the description of criminal states. Information currently available would suggest that only Equatorial Guinea, the Comoros and Seychelles could be correctly classified as criminal states. The majority of other African states illustrate classical symptoms of *la politique du ventre* (Senegal, Côte d'Ivoire, Gabon, Zimbabwe, Tanzania, Namibia) and certain may be said to produce more positive economic indicators (Ghana, Uganda, Botswana, Mali, Burkina Faso). Some states are clearly major organizers of smuggling (Gambia, Benin, Mozambique), but could not reasonably be described as criminal – although the precedent offered by Burundi, which for a long period was the smuggling capital of East and Central Africa, should warn us against complacency in this respect.

To be more precise, the relationship between the international economics of the drug trade and the political arena appears at present to be less intimate and less substantial than it is in Latin America or in certain Asian countries. When such a relationship does exist in a given African country, it is usually better understood as the manifestation of a classical tributary pattern rather than the sign of direct participation by political actors. There seems to be a direct relation between strategies of war or armed struggle and the sale or distribution of drugs, for example in Liberia and Sierra Leone, or to a lesser extent in Chad, Rwanda and Burundi, but there is no country south of the Sahara which, in this respect, is really comparable to Burma, Afghanistan or Peru. In some parts of Africa, the political class maintains relations with drug traders by way of the sons and daughters of those in power, such as in Zambia and Côte d'Ivoire, while, in South Africa, various militias or armed wings attached to political parties have a close acquaintance with the drug trade (see Chapter 3).

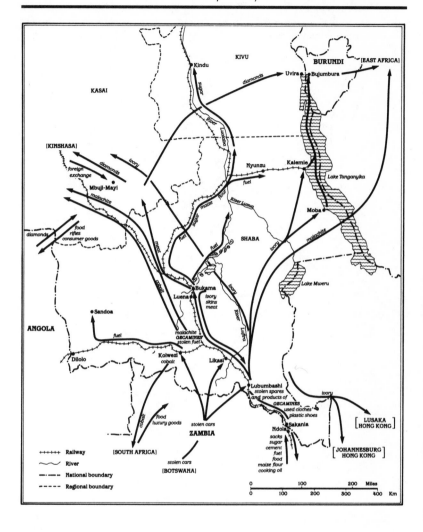

Figure 1.2   Principal commodities of unrecorded trade in south-east Zaïre
Source: Janet MacGaffey (ed.), *The Real Economy of Zaïre*, James Currey, London, 1991

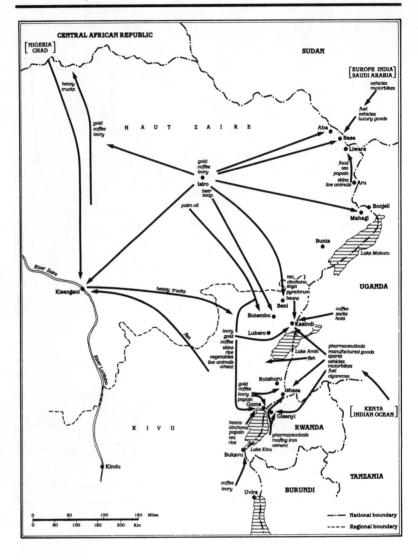

Figure 1.3 Principal commodities of unrecorded trade in north-east Zaïre
Source: Janet MacGaffey (ed.), *The Real Economy of Zaïre*, James Currey, London, 1991

The most interesting case is that of Nigeria. The US authorities have long been convinced, without ever being able to provide formal proof, that the armed forces, the political class and members of the government play a major role in Nigeria's drug trade. Prominent among the drug traders are Ibo networks, possibly working under the protection of various Northern groups. It is perhaps most likely that the Nigerian drug networks have maintained their relative autonomy and that the main factions which participate in the government of the country simply levy an unoffical tax or tithe on drugs which transit via Nigeria and charge the traders for various services, while drawing the greater part of their personal revenue from other sectors, especially oil. The drug trade is said to be viewed with disdain by the leading aristocratic families of the North which have dominated the country's politics since independence, or at least by the older generation among them. The military establishment cannot be shown to have been directly compromised other than by the participation in the international cocaine trade of the wife of a former head of state, herself from a rather dubious background, who was able to use her great political influence to protect various criminal entrepreneurs without undue attention from the law enforcement agencies. The country's leading drug enforcement agency is believed to have simply drawn its own unoffical tax from such a well-protected trade. If it is indeed the case that the political class maintains a certain distance from professional drug-trading organizations, this does not preclude the observation that a large part of the Nigerian economy and of Nigerian society is irrigated by the profits of the drug trade, in a similar way to what has happened in Colombia. If this is true, the political class would certainly not be excepted from the general rule governing the country as a whole.

The relative autonomy of merchant networks which are obliged to maintain a tributary relationship with those who wield political power, but which are also able in turn to exercise influence over holders of office or tenants of political power generally, may also be detected in Senegal. Here, this has grown out of the long historical alliance, nowadays under threat of rupture or estrangement, between the Socialist Party and the Mouride brotherhood or, in slightly different form, in the relations built up over years in the Central African Republic, former Zaïre, Zambia and other parts of Central Africa between trade networks dominated by foreigners of West African, Lebanese, Indian and Pakistani origin and the various national political authorities. Once again, in all of these cases, there is no configuration which could accurately be said to amount to the criminalization of the state.

If we refer to the six criteria enumerated above, we may observe that even a rapid analysis of the manner and degree of Africa's insertion in the international drug economy is not such as to permit the conclusion that the process has reached its logical final point. Holders of power may indeed, in some places and on some occasions, become accomplices in the narcotics trade. They use force, if necessary by using for private purposes the official organs of state coercion, to protect themselves and their protégés from over-zealous investigators. They are associated more or less closely with international networks of organized crime. They frequently form part of syndicates of power-brokers which we have described as a national board of directors, some of whose members remain in the shadows. However, it does not appear that, at present, holders of political office in Africa, who in a country like Nigeria are far from having a real monopoly of power, are using their position systematically for rational, large-scale participation in the drug trade. Moreover, the drug trade seems to remain secondary to more tested forms of predation and fraud which arise from the control of natural resources (especially oil) and of the import–export trade, and from the regular receipt of commissions derived from relations of various sorts with the outside world. The comparative advantage of sub-Saharan Africa in the production and processing of narcotics or in the laundering of drug profits is not as yet of such a type and scale as to be established beyond any shadow of doubt (see Chapter 4).

Seen through the prism of the drug trade, the criminalization of the state south of the Sahara has not yet reached its apogee. However, the potential for such a development is certainly present, particularly as the legacy represented by the existing practice of *la politique du ventre* implies that further immersion in the drug trade could take place without any great rupture with recent historical tradition. Concentration on the drug trade alone, which is no more than the most spectacular manifestation of a tangled shrubbery of illicit activity, should not blind us to the existence of a mass of other historically constituted dispositions which make Africa well suited to the further criminalization of its political institutions and its economic practices. But all of this remains far from inevitable. It is more helpful to view events and their potential in the light of historical continuity than in that of a 'great transformation'.

It must be said that the multiplication of conflicts, the main political logic of which is simple predation and which tend to be accompanied by a growing insertion in the international economy of illegality, as in the case of Chad, Liberia and Sierra Leone, the spread of a culture of institutional neglect, systematic plunder of the national economy and the uncontrolled privatization of the state (for example in former Zaïre, Kenya, Cameroon, Congo, Guinea, Togo, Central African Republic, São Tomé, Madagascar and Zambia) all suggest that a slide towards criminalization throughout the sub-continent is a strong probability. The examples of India, Colombia, Peru, Turkey, Russia and perhaps Japan and Italy demonstrate that neither centralization of government nor the democracy of the market is sufficient to insulate any society against such an eventuality.

For what it is worth, the establishment of a statistical measure of the degree of criminalization of politics in Africa – a mark out of ten, say – is less useful than an analysis of the historical origins of the process and a reconstruction of the sequence of events which has brought it into being. The diversity of the situations we have considered suggests that such sequences are largely contingent, just as, in its time, was the rise of the Camorra in Naples, which was able to exploit the rise of the drug market in the 1970s and to embezzle massive amounts of state aid provided after the earthquake of 1980, in a structural context of political clientelism, the prevalence of an informal economy and the dependence of the region of Campagna on public resources (Cesoni, 1995). South of the Sahara, the increasingly evident interaction between the formation of the state, the primitive accumulation of capital, war, and illicit economic activity has its origin in the specific experiences of societies as much as in their degree of contact with the international economy of crime. For this reason the process of criminalization assumes different forms from one African society to another, or between one network and another.

2

The 'Social Capital' of the Felonious State

or the Ruses of Political Intelligence

JEAN-FRANÇOIS BAYART

For ease of reference, this chapter will use the term 'social capital' to refer to the ensemble of configurations and the texture of relationships which are the outcome of sub-Saharan Africa's long historical trajectory, or rather of the cluster of historical trajectories, distinct but acting upon one another over long periods, of an entire sub-continent. The term 'social capital' has been borrowed from a specialist on Italy, Robert D. Putnam, who himself discovered it in the works of two renowned Africanists, James Coleman and Robert Bates. The use made of this concept by Putnam to analyse the governance of the Italian peninsula has captured the imagination of World Bank experts, even if it has not convinced every specialist on Italian affairs. Some political analysts, in fact, have published trenchant criticisms of their Harvard colleague. For present purposes, it is necessary to take note of these criticisms and to purge the notion of 'social capital' of the connotation of determinism which has been the chief ground on which it has been contested. We may accept that the concept 'refers to features of social organization, such as trust, norms, and networks, that can improve the efficiency of society by facilitating coordinated actions: like other forms of capital, social capital is productive, making possible the achievement of certain ends that would not be attainable in its absence' (Putnam, 1993: 167). But, if we are to use the expression at all, it is vital to make clear that it should not be taken to postulate the existence of an 'African culture' which is static and resistant to change over time, as so many commentators have maintained, most notably writers on the ethno-development which is nowadays so much in vogue at the World Bank. Rather, we would emphasize the abundance of distinct and sometimes contradictory cultural repertoires, at the same time stable and subject to change, which are vehicles of both transformation and continuity. Considered in this light, such repertoires are inseparable from the ongoing development of personal or particular histories, since the making of history continues in contemporary Africa, and is not peculiar to ancient Africa only.

More fundamentally, we need to reconsider the real fabric of African history, or rather of African histories, which is characterized by an extreme mobility and adaptability both in geographical space and in cultural matters. In the absence of almost any personalized system of written codification of land tenure outside Ethiopia, the relation between political and economic territory in Africa was for many centuries a highly fluid one, and identities which would today be described as ethnic or religious were subjects of permanent negotiation and renegotiation. It is in this sense that old Africa has been described as a 'frontier continent', in the American sense (Kopytoff, 1987a). The process of colonization, and the formation of a bureaucratic state sited in a defined territory which this set in motion, did not eliminate older patterns in most of sub-Saharan Africa even if the process led to a reification or 'fixing' of ethnic awareness, in the opinion of most anthropologists and historians. Even today, it has been aptly said that 'no condition is permanent', in regard to either socioeconomics or identity (Berry, 1993).

The criminalization of the political societies and the economies of the sub-continent, if indeed it comes about, can occur only as the product of specific historical experiences and of the 'social capital' which these have created. Without pretending to be exhaustive, we shall examine how several features of the existing 'social capital' are such as may facilitate the interaction of politics and crime south of the Sahara. Nevertheless, it is worth repeating one further time that Africa does not have a monopoly of 'social capital' of this type and that the translation of such a heritage into a specific configuration of crime and politics, if that is what transpires, owes a great deal to historical contingencies such as the current economic crisis, the failure of structural adjustment, and the development of an international economy of crime. These historical contingencies are the factors which precipitate, in the chemical meaning of the word, the transformation of la *politique du ventre*. It should also be said that the 'social capital' created by Africa's past can lead to a future other than one characterized by crime, since the same cultural representations can serve various schemas of social action. Ethnicity, for example, which we have described as providing an element of cohesion to drug-trafficking networks and enabling them to prosper, can also serve as the inspiration for a true 'moral economy' of politics, such as a historian of Kenya, John Lonsdale, has demonstrated with remarkable insight. Ethnicity provides the ground for legitimizing both corruption and its denunciation.

Ambivalence is a key element of both political and social action (Bayart, 1996: 166 *et seq.*). This observation is conspicuously true in regard to criminality, since criminal organizations so often claim to articulate rigorous moral codes, such as the Sicilian Mafia code of honour. Leading violators of the law frequently display more than a casual interest in edifying moral discourses. Agha Hasan Abedi, founder of the Bank of Credit and Commerce International (BCCI), saw his bank as both a family and a secret society, reflected in the pseudo-philosophical jargon and the various rituals associated with the company. He established the Third World Foundation, publisher both of the *Third World Quarterly*, a review modelled on the prestigious American publication *Foreign Affairs*, and the magazine *South*, notable for its crusading approach to questions of world development. He was a generous donor to the Carter Presidential Center in Atlanta, Georgia, and a still more generous contributor to the non-profit-making organization Global 2000, set up by the former president of the United States, Jimmy Carter, to run projects on health and rural development, notably in Africa. In the most extreme cases, crime actually flourishes in the bosom of religion: bandits can be assiduous in undertaking pious works (thus giving rise to the notion that they can be 'social'), and in the Ottoman Empire or nineteenth-century India outlaws were commonly graduates of Koranic schools or former members of ascetic brotherhoods. Illicit activities undertaken by an individual can serve to further that same person's social promotion and respect. In Ethiopia, the *sheftenat*, the institution of banditry, permitted people of low status to rise in the social hierarchy and minor nobles to acquire greater political standing. In the same way prostitution has been, since the beginning of the present century, a means by which more than a few women have cared for their families, contributed to the life of their villages, and started businesses.

The cultural repertoires of social mobility

A first series of ethical schemas to be found in the 'social capital' of Africa appears to display a marked affinity with the spirit of criminality as we have described it. Contrary to what is often said, African societies are characterized less by their communalism than by the almost frenetic individualism of those who comprise them. It is certainly the case that African societies feature strong collective constraints which are enforced by political or judicial institutions endowed with considerable powers of coercion. Nevertheless, individuals can and do ceaselessly strive to improve themselves, including in the political arena. The basic myths of many African societies, their founding charters so to speak, are full of stories of heroes who have emerged from the wild bush and who take control of a kingdom by virtue of their personal powers of performance in war, hunting, magic and love. In different circumstances, the same is true of the political existence of modern states: we need do no more than consider the biographies of so many of the founding fathers of modern Africa, who started from obscure origins and finally climbed to the top of the greasy pole of politics by struggling against the colonizer or by collaborating with him. In so-called independent religious movements also, prophets are frequently outsiders of this sort, but it is in the field of the accumulation of wealth that entrepreneurs starting from humble origins are to be found *par excellence*. The biographies of the leading businessmen and women in Africa today are as edifying as those of the great self-made American business magnates, provided only that one set aside the knowledge of just how important political connections have been for business success in the rent-seeking economies of postcolonial Africa. Even the career of someone as well known and as wealthy as Moshood Abiola, undoubtedly the true winner of the 1993 presidential election in Nigeria, had an element of the unexplained and inexplicable.

Africans are true frontiersmen, in the sense of being imbued with the pioneer spirit. The famous *sapeurs*, the young dandies of Brazzaville, use the word 'adventure' to describe their journey of initiation to Paris. The Somalian businesswomen and Togolese *nana-benz* who thrive in the import–export trade, Nigerian and Congolese currency dealers and speculators, Malian migrant workers, and the young men who risk their lives in the search for diamonds, gold or other precious stones or metals in a growing number of countries all show an even greater sense of adventure. South of the Sahara, social and even physical existence is inconceivable without the concepts of daring and risk-taking. Illustrations of this may be found in the notion of money as the reward for the successful pursuit of chance: monetary fortune has to be pursued as a hunter pursues his quarry, in situations where exchange rates are exceptionally volatile and inflation rates high, and where bank notes are sometimes nicknamed 'dead leaves'. Further illustrations may be found in sexual and amorous experiences which are pursued in the shadow of death by participants in the system of *bureaugamie*[1] (for the wealthy) and common debauchery (for diggers in the diamond camps).

This unbridled sense of individualism and adventure is related to at least two cultural repertoires, connected one to the other, which appear

---

[1] A Congolese expression coming from the expression 'Office number two' ['*deuxième bureau*'], applied to the mistresses of politicians and senior officials. In many cases there are in fact Offices numbers three and four as well as number two.

to underpin the practice of criminality in contemporary Africa, including urban delinquency and the drug trade. One such repertoire is that of myth and folk tales, which to this day is one of the main forms in which children are socialized and educated, and the other is that of the invisible, which pervades all social, political and economic life.

In the corpus of African folk tales, studied most notably by Denise Paulme, the Trickster plays a central role in various forms, such as in the person of the Hare, the Spider, or the human child endowed with particular cunning. The Trickster is an ambiguous character, 'creative, but clumsy and given to blunders', who 'succeeds in performing some "impossible" labour only to fail at the last moment'. 'In folk tales, trickery wins the day only when it is used to save the innnocent, denounce the guilty or punish an offence.' The Trickster is by definition one who shows ability in 'turning circumstances to his advantage and in particular in having others take his place, creating a situation in his own interest', and is further defined by his 'flexibility', his 'duplicity', his 'inversion of habitual values', his 'cunning'. Much appreciated by any African audience, the figure of the Trickster nevertheless evokes 'complex feelings' of admiration, irritation and caution because of the ambivalent and often reprehensible manner in which he behaves (Paulme, 1976). Denise Paulme herself makes a comparison between the qualities of the Trickster and that known to the ancient Greeks as *mètis,* whose connection with the techniques of hunting and fishing is clear:

> In every situation of adversity or competition ... success may be obtained by either of two methods. On the one hand, it may be obtained by superior 'power' in whatever constitutes the field of struggle, in which victory goes to the strongest. But, on the other hand, success may be obtained by techniques of a different order entirely, whose purpose is to change the apparent outcome of the struggle and to give victory to the one who appeared to have been defeated. In this way success obtained by means of *mètis* carries a connotation of ambiguity: according to the context, it can excite differing emotional reactions. In some circumstances, one may detect in its exercise the workings of an intent to deceive, since the rules of the game have been flouted. In other circumstances, it is seen as all the more admirable in that it contains an element of surprise, whereby the weaker party, against all expectations, finds sufficient inner strength to defeat the stronger. Certain aspects of the notion of *mètis* bring to mind ideas of treacherous deception, lying with perfidious intent, betrayal, the strategems of women and cowards. But in slightly different contexts it is more prized than power itself. *Mètis* is in a sense the ultimate weapon, the only one which can be used successfully in all circumstances, whatever the rules of the

game, to achieve victory, or the domination of one person by another (Detienne and Vernant, 1974: 19–20).

In many respects the notion of *mètis* is a useful tool with which to consider politics and economics in modern Africa, with its lexicon of trickery and sudden changes of alliance and the frequency of social redistribution, of shameless social parasitism and cynical appropriation. Didier Bigo (1988: chap. 6) has already remarked on the striking similarity between the figure of the Emperor Bokassa in the Central African Republic and the Trickster in the pantheon of Banda belief. Insofar as it is permissible to accord a preponderant role at the heart of the postcolonial state to the practice of straddling – simultaneously occupying positions of power and positions of accumulation – and to the importance of factional struggle, this insight deserves to be considered in a wider context. Political and economic actors in Africa often demonstrate some of the characteristics of the Trickster of folk tales. This description certainly fits those agents of the process of criminalization who, for example, are active in the drug trade or in financial fraud, whose social profile is at least as ambiguous as that of the Trickster, and who may sometimes be popularly viewed as 'heroic criminals' (Austen, 1986).

If it is indeed true that '*mètis* is dominant in every sphere of activity in which man must learn to deal with hostile powers or forces too potent to be controlled directly, but which can nevertheless be made useful, without ever confronting them head-on, in order to succeed in a plan through mechanisms of improvisation' (Detienne and Vernant, 1974: 57), then it becomes easy to imagine the extent to which this quality is required in Africa, whose degree of dependence on the rest of the world has increased over the last two decades and whose states remain apparatuses for the acquisition of plunder. In these circumstances, *mètis* is a component of a moral universe which is shared by the senior civil servant who uncovers a way around the conditionality imposed by foreign aid donors, and by the drug courier, the modern-day Trickster who has to negotiate his – or often her – way past the customs officers of London's Heathrow or New York's JFK airport. It is shared too by the lady of the night who uses the revenue gained from her profession to maintain a family or to provide the start-up capital for a business.

The second major repertoire used in the service of highly individualistic enterprises involving a massive degree of personal risk is that of the invisible which, in the societies of precolonial Africa, was already a fertile ground of social ascension. Although this implies far more than just the use of witchcraft, the latter is an important component of the world of invisible forces and spirits. As a realm of the cultural imagination, the field of witchcraft is a powerful communicator of idioms of the market economy, of which it is itself an element, as the anthropologist Peter Geschiere, a specialist on Cameroon, has demonstrated. In particular, the accumulation of wealth has given rise to new forms of witchcraft, such as *ekong* in Cameroon, which equate enrichment with the 'eating' of the Other or at least with the utter subjection of the Other to the witch's will in the invisible world. The notion of *la politique du ventre* contains an implicit reference to such beliefs or such symbolizations of human relationships. Criminals, like other social actors, work in the dimension of the invisible, and this is also very important in warfare, including in modern war. Young fighters in Liberia and Nigerian drug couriers both use a related system of representations. But in this respect they are no different from the many heads of state who surround themselves with marabouts of dubious reputation, manipulate spiritual forces to protect themselves or attack their enemies, and organize themselves in such secret societies as Freemasonry, Rosicrucianism, the Prima Curia and Transcendental Meditation. Politicians bring to associations of this sort a specific esoteric and sometimes bloody element, an explanation for the rise in ritual murders which seems to be taking place in several countries along the West African coast. Such practices and such structures are at the heart of factional intrigues in Cameroon, Gabon and Mozambique, for example. Testimonies of acts of Satanism, such as in former Zaïre, are also increasing, and here it is relevant to note that pacts with the Devil are widely believed to be a means of ensuring wealth and worldly success.

Here again, the view that such practices represent an essential continuity with the past rather than a radical break in the system of values seems very persuasive. Most of the tendencies we have described existed already at the time of Africa's independence. They were, however, hidden from view by the ideology of nationalism and by the conviction that such manifestations of 'tradition' were fated to disappear with progress. Nowadays, it is easier to see that these representations, on the contrary, constitute an idiom for articulating social change. Moreover, from a cultural point of view – and it will be seen in due course that the same is true from an economic viewpoint – legal and institutional practice is underpinned by the same world-view as practices sometimes described as informal or as those which are clearly criminal in nature. The businessman whose company is registered with the government registrar, the peddler in the streets of the poorer parts of town, the opportunist thief who accompanies him, the digger of diamonds and the trafficker in heroin, all cultivate spiritual powers to increase their chance of success and enhance their use of the quality of *mètis*. 'We live mysteriously', Zaïreans often used to say to explain the workings of their country's economy. In fact, the person who struggles daily to survive and who, using the energy and the spirit of survival called by the citizens of Kinshasa *débrouillardise*, the local name for *mètis*, supplies the city with food and distributes fuel to the provinces is no different in essence from the diamond digger or the cocaine courier. In the name of the same ethos of personal savoir-faire and initiative, he passes from one activity to another. Only the vision of the jurist imposes a difference between these categories, labelling one criminal and another not, a distinction without meaning to the vast mass of those in pursuit of social betterment and religious salvation.

The 'social capital' of organizations

There is a second series of repertoires constituting the 'social capital' which Africa derives from its past. According to prevailing circumstances, the societies of old Africa were on occasion highly institutionalized, and on occasion dominated by warlords who imposed their rule by the most brutal force, with both modes of government co-existing or succeeding one another within the same polity in many cases. But however great the degree of centralization of power around one person or one set of state institutions, or even around a sophisticated national constitution, as was the case with Ashanti in the eighteenth and nineteenth centuries, the institution of the kinship lineage remained an effective unit. In some cases lineages were the mainstay of society, either because no autonomous structure of power had emerged, or because the collapse of a central state left the lineage unchallenged as the basis of social order. In other words, the logic of lineage systems is not antithetical to that of the state, as was often believed in the past. The two can co-exist and even prosper together. In fact, lineage-based societies have often proved to have a surprising capacity to adapt to new bureaucratic environments and to market economies. This is precisely the case with the Ibo of Nigeria, whose segmentary system has abundantly proved its affinity with the market mechanism. The success of Ibo networks in the drug trade is only one illustration of a much more widespread commercial success.

The 'moral economy' of ethnicity, which is often in reality a moral economy of the kinship group, has developed 'civic traditions',[2] and in particular sentiments of solidarity and business confidence, whose most highly developed practical technique is that of the *tontine* or savings club. This is certainly not based on any sentiment of 'affection', as Goran Hyden (1980) suggested in a rather unfortunate misnomer, but

---

[2] We are here explicitly using the term employed by Robert Putnam with reference to northern Italy.

on elaborate notions of trust. This principle is so widespread that oligopolies in African markets, which are sources of lucrative profits particularly in the import–export trade, sometimes give rise to veritable guilds, a phenomenon probably at its most complex in Nigeria. It is hardly necessary to point out that such a form of economic organization, with a lack of transparency which makes it ideally suited to fraud and smuggling, can easily lend itself to criminal enterprises. In Nigeria the financial frauds known as '419' are said to be run by members of such a guild, and we have already discussed the comparative advantage which Ibo drug traders are able to derive from the social capital of the kinship lineage.

In the same way, sodalities of initiates flourish in certain lineage societies, for example in the form of societies of human lions, panthers and leopards. They represent countervailing centres of power, which may be seen as either legitimate or deviant in nature, such as on occasions when they engage in banditry or political terrorism. Max Weber accurately compared such sodalities to the Mafia, the Camorra, and the Chinese secret societies. They are well equipped to provide the protection identified by writers on organized crime, and are even liable to create a need for protection which they themselves then propose to satisfy. It is notable, for example, that the importance of the Poro society appears to have greatly increased in Liberia and Sierra Leone in the context of civil war in both countries.

The kinship mode of organization has all the same characteristics as the shadow structures of power which are currently so much in evidence at the national level. The primacy of notables or other community leaders within a given lineage is, by definition, relative and dependent on circumstances. It depends on the quality of individual performance in any given situation and is subject to constant evaluation, discussion, negotiation and contestation on the part of other elders, social juniors and in particular women, who play a role through various rituals, in the manner of the chorus in a Greek tragedy. Moreover, lineage societies often contain two hierarchical systems, those representing the descendants of conquerors and those representing the descendants of the first settlers of an area, who may claim powers, for example one over the heavens and the other over the earth, and which are obliged to compromise constantly with one another as a means of regulating their on-going rivalries. Colonization accentuated the effects of having a twin system of power by imposing a new line of authority, that of the administrative chiefs who, although officially dubbed 'traditional leaders', were none the less new creations and were often recruited from the lower levels of society. In other words, in lineage societies the exercise of power is subject to deliberations in secret conclave. Groups of this sort soon came to wield influence in the postcolonial state through the regional affiliations of members of the national political elite. This does not, of course, mean that the modern African state is no more than a conspiracy of greybearded old men. Nevertheless, the leaders of the army and the one-party state who ruled Congo-Brazzaville from 1968 to 1991, generally having their roots in the north of the country, always showed themselves most attentive to the complaints they received from whichever specific area they came from, in the course of their frequent political tours. The 'board of directors' which surrounded President Lissouba while he was president of Congo was no more than an extension of this mode of government, in this case under the influence of a 'nibolek' clique rather than a coterie of northerners. In similar vein, in Cameroon, the 'Beti lobby', which is occupied in plundering the state in the shadow of President Biya, operates at the interface where the lineage societies of the Centre-South and the South meet the country's formal political institutions.

Two other forms of social organization are nowadays becoming prominent, which owe little to the lineage form of organization and may even be said to transcend it. The first of these is armed movements, whose degree of ethnic cohesiveness is often exaggerated and which recruit, by force if necessary, young people from a great variety of social backgrounds. These recruits are required, or forced, to cut their links with their families. What they acquire is access to the international trade economy, to the world of the city and, in the case of young males, to that rarest of all commodities, young women. The second emerging form of social organization is prophetic, sectarian and neo-fundamentalist religious movements, Christian or Islamic, which are means of social advancement or, at any rate, of economic survival for their leaders and which offer them access to public space and even a range of international contacts. In reordering their members' lines of social identification and in giving birth to new basic communities – the guerrilla group or the armed movement for young combatants, the church or the religious assembly for religious believers – such organizations, which fit into a well-defined pattern of African history, are important avenues of social change and affect the manner in which African societies articulate with those in other parts of the world. For example, the Mouride brotherhood specializes in the import–export trade, Christian sects in east Kasai attract members from among communities of diamond diggers and themselves export diamonds, and African immigrants in Western Europe organize themselves into religious communities, including Islamic ones, but also and perhaps more importantly Christian and syncretic ones whose commercial activities should not be underestimated, even if they have been the subject of little research. As for the armed movements, they generally finance themselves by drawing profits from the imports and exports of the zones which they control and by subjecting foreign operatives to different forms of tax or tribute, as in Angola, Liberia or Somalia.

It goes without saying that each of these two categories of organization is well placed to participate in activities considered as criminal by the international community, while itself enunciating religious or political grounds for regarding such activities as legitimate. This is already an established practice for armed movements south of the Sahara, which have developed a veritable political economy of war founded on the informal and the illicit, but the same tendency could soon become apparent in the case of religious movements. According to the rather scarce data at our disposal, some are already implicated in illegal activity including the drug trade. Operating in both Ghana and Nigeria, one Christian church procures false passports for its members and advances the cost of their passage to New York, some $3,000, which the travellers have to repay. In the same way, the Mourides appear to have some acquaintance with the narcotics traffic in the countries of the Mediterranean rim. This sort of development is hardly unique, since several large international religious organizations are well known as money launderers and agents of financial gain of a fraudulent, abusive, or frankly criminal nature.

The historical experiences of the last two centuries

The cultural repertoires and the types of social organization which most easily lend themselves to the criminalization of African economies cannot be considered in isolation from the historical experiences which the sub-continent has undergone over the past two centuries. It is worth repeating that these experiences have not given rise to an abstract 'social capital' which is manifested in an equally abstract 'African culture'. Rather, 'social capital' and culture are the epiphenomena or the expressions of the historical trajectory of a sub-continent whose main characteristics have included a limited development of its productive capacity, a limited degree of social and cultural polarization, and a relatively feeble amount of political and administrative centralization as a result of social struggles, ecological or demographic constraints, and foreign interference.

As far as Africa is concerned, the main consequence of this line of development over the long term has been its progressively greater degree of dependence. This has taken various forms over time, beginning with the slave trade, passing through colonization and finding its current expression in the loss of a sovereignty only recently acquired at the time of independence. We may recall that this dependence has often been created by Africans anxious to assert their control over others within their own societies, or, on the other hand, by people seeking to break the domination of those who enjoyed a monopoly of cultural or commercial relations with the external world to the benefit of specific sectors of the population. In other words, numerous social groups in Africa have built their strategies on a situation of dependence, and the most successful among them have drawn handsome rents from it, in the form of financial and material benefits. Examples of attempts to turn external constraints into instruments of domestic political or economic control include participation in different branches of the slave trade controlled by European or Muslim traders, collaboration with colonial powers, the diplomatic and military alliances of the Cold War, the internalization of the dogma of structural adjustment (although not the spirit underlying it), the adoption of the rhetoric of democratization, and what might be termed 'NGO-itis'.

Historically, strategies to manage dependence have given rise to political and economic forms whose affinities with a putative process of criminalization are highly instructive. In the political domain, large areas of Africa have in the past been dominated by wars for long periods, especially in the later nineteenth century, largely because of a boom in the slave trade in the Nile Valley and the Indian Ocean rim, and in the last two hundred years have known only relatively brief periods of peace. Here, we should be careful not to overestimate the advantages brought by colonization. For one consequence of colonization was to lead Africa into two world wars in which it had to make a heavy sacrifice. Moreover the 'pacification' so vaunted by colonial ideologues came about only late in the day. In many parts of Africa military administrations and martial law were lifted only after the Second World War, and rebellions were endemic. In 1928, for example, a rising of the Gbaya in Oubangui-Chari threatened to spread to all of French Equatorial Africa. In 1934, a massive peasant rising shook Burundi. In Ethiopia, the Italian occupation did not succeed in putting an end to the institution of *sheftenat*. From the 1940s and in later decades, European sovereignty was once more contested by armed movements in several countries (Madagascar, Kenya, Cameroon, Angola, Mozambique, Guinea-Bissau, Zimbabwe and South Africa). Last but not least, in the first years of independence, there were many military confrontations in the form of social or millenarian rebellions such as in Congo-Léopoldville, Nigeria and Chad, or of clashes between organizations arising out of the anticolonial struggle (Angola and Mozambique) or stemming from political and regional dissidence (Sudan, Eritrea, Nigeria, Uganda, Somalia), and there have been social or ethnic conflicts sometimes amounting to genocide, as in Rwanda and Burundi. Inasmuch as the *pax britannica* or the *paix coloniale* ever existed at all, it was no more than a brief parenthesis in a history haunted by the spectre of war.

War, however, does not represent the mechanical expression of a social order mired in tradition or primitiveness, nor is it the simple result of ethnic or regional rivalries. Military activity has always been associated in Africa, as in the rest of the world, with change and even with modernization, and it has always been one of the main vehicles for the recomposition of identities, whether political, ethnic or religious, at the same time as it has been one of the main ways in which African societies have assumed a position in international affairs. Today this remains true of those major conflicts which are contributing to the large-scale spread of modern weapons, the reshaping of ethnic identities, the remaking of relationships between sexes and generations, the spread of cultural symbols of foreign origin, the development of the import–export economy and even of salaried employment and regular payment of taxes. Perhaps what is really at stake in these conflicts is less the disintegration of the state, but the opposite, its formation. If this is indeed so, the wars of the Great Lakes region could be the contemporary equivalent of the massive upheavals caused by the *mfecane* after the victory of King Shaka's Zulu kingdom in the early years of the nineteenth century. With the advantage of hindsight we can perhaps see more clearly that the perennial occurrence of war as a factor of social innovation, political regulation and economic exchange is a historical thread, including what one might call the 'privatization' of military activity. The Zambezia region of Mozambique was, in the nineteenth century, divided into autonomous or independent *prazos* controlled by mixed-blood or Asian *senhores* who dabbled in the slave trade by means of personal armies composed of slave-warriors known as *achikunda*. In the same way in Ethiopia, and especially in the province of Tigray, the institution of *sheftenat* enabled local feudal lords and bandit chiefs to negotiate the terms of their own co-optation by the central government, without their acts of rebellion remotely threatening the unity of the empire. The current articulation between the specific political economy of so-called low-intensity conflicts and the internationalization of organized crime, if indeed it develops in the way we have suggested as likely, would be no more than an illustration of the reappearance of this mode of government.

Dazzled by the nationalist paradigm which was legitimated by critiques of colonialism and by the still recent independence of African states, academics and development policy officials and experts have given insufficient attention to the very rapid revival of mercantilist and predatory economies in some parts of the continent. As early as 1963, a European customs officer in Congo-Léopoldville observed a caravan of 500 porters, with armed escort, crossing the frontier between North Kivu and Uganda, illegally exporting agricultural goods to what were described as 'Ismaili smugglers'. In 1964, according to one author, an estimated 10 to 12 million carats of diamonds were exported illegally from Congo, some 81 per cent of official production (MacGaffey, 1987: 117 *et seq.*). With the large-scale revival of commercial routes of this sort, often along the lines of those traced in the nineteenth century, the main geopolitical axes of Africa are once more being contested. Thus, the eastern provinces of Chad and the Central African Republic, under pressure from the activities of guerrilla fighters, clerics, traders and poachers from the Sudan, are clearly coming back into the orbit of the valley of the Nile from which they were detached, in a highly artificial manner, by French colonial rule. A return to the economic sphere of influence of the Nile valley seems all the more inevitable since the attempt to link these areas into an Atlantic trading system never did take firm root, for lack of sufficient investment. In a similar way, the wars of the Great Lakes region will determine whether the east of the Democratic Republic of Congo is attached to an Indian Ocean economic zone or to the lower Congo basin, although informal trade – and the state of the roads – has for many years turned the trade of the entire area towards the east rather than the west.

There is another sphere in which the brief parenthesis of the colonial period has not disturbed Africa's older historical patterns as much as has sometimes been said. Rather than having little or no recourse to forced labour as a technique for mobilizing manpower, European colonial authorities intensified and systematized the use of coercion, either by making use of chartered companies whose abuses, especially in central Africa, have left a mark on those societies up to the present day, or by delegating the power of coercion to auxiliary administrative authorities who were equally harsh in their treatment of the general population. Forced labour was abolished only late in the colonial period – in 1945 in the French colonies – and in reality it continued to be established practice in some rural areas until independence. The nationalist elites which then took power sometimes renewed practices of this type under the guise of 'human investment', for example in the Central African Republic and Congo, and also in Tanzania, or they allowed certain administrative personnel to do so, such as in the area governed by the lamido or chief of Rey Bouba and in many administrative areas of north Cameroon. In some respects the long thread of forced labour has never been completely broken south of the Sahara, and its use by various military movements today should be understood in this context.

Colonization was based on a third element of historical continuity which the nationalist elites came to assume in their turn. The relatively small number of European officials ruled Africa by making use of indigenous intermediaries on whom they were heavily dependent, if only for linguistic reasons. The precise way in which this arrangement worked varied greatly from one place to another. Sometimes, the local intermediaries were powerful social hierarchies, as in the north of Nigeria or in most of the kingdoms of the Great Lakes. In other cases, they were created out of nothing by the co-optation of newcomers, particularly in lineage-based societies without any tradition of centralized political institutions. This mode of government was more or less codified, and even if the British were the only ones to push it to its logical extreme in the form of the doctrine of Indirect Rule, all colonial administration was in reality indirect and relied on autochtonous elites for its mediation. In this respect, colonial rule constituted a formidable historical experience of deceipt, duplicity and treachery, which some anthropologists have euphemistically called the 'working misunderstandings' on which European occupation was based (Bayart, 1993: 283 n. 108). It was, by the same token, an extraordinary academy for improvization and *mètis*, of which interpreters, office-messengers, clerks and catechists became the picaresque and often 'dishonest' heroes. 'Ambiguous Africa', Georges Balandier called this in the 1950s.

Above all, the colonial situation provided the occasion for a wide range of practices of fraudulent accumulation of wealth by these auxiliary Tricksters who profited from their function as political and cultural intermediaries for economic gain. Hence, the organization of forced labourers, the levying of taxes, the registration of property in official censuses and registers, and access to formal legal services and to bank loans were systematically used in the service of private interests and to a great degree prefigured what was later to be called 'corruption' or 'the privatization of the state'. It goes without saying that the nationalist movements were no strangers to this development. This was all the more so because certain of them, for example in South Africa or in Kenya at the time of Mau Mau, maintained a close relationship with the criminal underworld, even if this connection between revolutionary activism and banditry seems to have been less marked south of the Sahara than it was in the Italy of the *Risorgimento*, the Balkans under Ottoman rule, Tsarist Russia or Republican China. Once ensconced in power, nationalist organizations, transformed by more or less violent means into single parties, reorganized for the benefit of their officials and more particularly their leaders the profits derived from rents acquired in the tenure of official or political office, in most cases transforming themselves into machines at the service of a *nomenklatura* and, in a few cases, such as the Parti démocratique de Guinée, into authentic fraternities of crime. In many cases, young people were mobilized as an auxiliary force whose excesses, for example in Burundi, Congo-Brazzaville and Malawi, occasionally served as advance warning of the outrages which were to be perpetrated by the militias of the 1990s.

It is relevant to note that organizations of a mafia type in southern Italy have prospered precisely in activities of mediation of this sort, for example in the labour market or in the allocation of public resources. The colonial legacy of indirect rule, perpetuated in the way in which a bureaucracy acquires habits of command in a specified territory and in the networks of influence and clientelism which constitute the post-colonial state, like a rhizome in its tangled complexity, in all probability makes African political societies predisposed to criminal activity.

From this point of view, the alternation between single-party or military regimes and periods of relative political freedom and multi-party activity, or the occurrence of a period of state-centred and nationalist dirigisme succeeded by one of liberalization and privatization, is a relatively unimportant factor. From the beginning it is one and the same principle which has prevailed: that of the trade in influence, to the extent that one may wonder whether influence has not itself been turned into a form of merchandise over the last few decades, at the same time as it has become militarized in certain situations and 'democratized' in others.

In the following chapters, the study of two specific cases will help us to understand this process better. In South Africa, the massive growth of crime, the development of connections with various foreign 'mafias', the privatization of violence by the securocrats of the armed forces and the National Party, but also by officials of the ANC and Inkatha and by the township shacklords who attempt to control markets in housing and transport, are all phenomena indissociable from the historical experiences of indirect rule, of the ruthless housing and employment practices of the mining economy, of racial segregation, of urbanization, banditry, and the struggle both to maintain and to overthrow apartheid (Chapter 3). Similarly, the analysis of the actual way in which African economies have functioned over the last century seems to support the hypothesis of a continuity rather than a rupture between the historical patterns of the nineteenth and twentieth centuries and what threatens to be, at the dawn of the next millennium, the process of insertion of the sub-continent into the criminal networks of the international system (see Chapter 4).

If this is indeed an accurate analysis, then two developments which are generally regarded by commentators and aid donors as pointers to the revival of sub-Saharan Africa, namely, the reintegration of South Africa into the concert of African nations and economic liberalization, risk having effects different from those predicted. In this respect the political developments of the current decade will have unusually far-reaching consequences, even if it is premature to draw definitive conclusions at the present stage. The use of criminal networks by political authorities desperate to revive their failing power, or even, in the most extreme cases, the militarization of entire societies and most particularly of the youth, may lead in time to a thoroughgoing organization of political criminality. A sinister precursor of this is perhaps the example of the camps controlled by the ex-Rwandan Armed Forces in the Great Lakes region in 1994–6. The spread of electoral politics is such that, in the context of clientelist systems, it multiplies the opportunities for that form of mediation which is most conducive to illicit activity, as the examples of the Mafia and the Camorra illustrate. The decentralization and the regionalization recommended by enthusiasts of 'good governance' and 'civil society' can entail similar consequences, at least to judge from the Italian and Russian cases. Last but not least, the constraints imposed by political and economic conditionality can lead holders of power to beat an orderly retreat to strategic niches of the criminal underworld, on the model pioneered by the KGB when its directors realized that the collapse of the USSR had become inevitable. Situated as they are in the longer history of the last two centuries, the sequences of economic and political liberalization in Africa no doubt hold in store some very odd forms of deregulation indeed.

3

The New Frontiers of Crime in South Africa

STEPHEN ELLIS

In warfare, according to the British field-marshal Lord Montgomery, 'the first principle is to identify your enemy accurately' (quoted in Prins and Stamp, 1991: 32).

South Africa today has no foreign enemies. Its government enjoys overwhelming national and international support. President Nelson Mandela is probably the world's most admired living politician. And yet the state, in the face of a multiplicity of armed groups, is incapable of enforcing the monopoly of legitimate violence which is its most fundamental responsibility, and this poses such a substantial threat to national security and stability that Montgomery's dictum remains relevant. Exactly who or what is responsible for the wave of crime which is affecting the country? An essential task of political analysis in these circumstances is to define the relationship between politics and the practices of illicit violence and illicit enrichment which we call crime.

It should be said at the outset that even a cursory examination of the recent history of South Africa indicates that organized crime has ceased to be a phenomenon at the fringes of political and economic society, the place traditionally allotted to it in the social sciences (cf. Waller and Yasmann, 1995: 277). South Africa is said to have the highest incidence of murder of any country in the world not at war. Half the population pronounce themselves in opinion polls to be 'very worried' about becoming victims of crime in their own communities (South African Police Service, 1996: 1). In just two years, 80 per cent of more than 2,000 households surveyed by the banking group Nedcor had had some experience of crime (Johnson, 1996). Sections of some black townships are effectively under the control of unofficial armed groups, sometimes in the guise of Self-Defence or Self-Protection Units claiming allegiance to the African National Congress (ANC) or the

Inkatha Freedom Party (IFP), or they are threatened by *tsotsis*, gang-sters with no political ideology. Gunmen carrying illegal weapons and operating on the margins between party militias, self-defence units, comrades and crime gangs are known, in the rich vocabulary of South African politics, as 'com-tsotsis', 'comrade-gangsters'. Weapons are readily available. An AK-47 assault rifle can be bought on the black market or even hired by the day, with or without bullets. The country's middle classes increasingly tend to live in enclaves patrolled by pri-vate security companies, behind high walls topped by razor wire. Free of the unwelcome attentions of armed militias, they are frequently worried by burglary and particularly by the high rate of vehicle theft – 98,000 vehicles in 1995 – sometimes carried out by armed hijackers who lie in wait by the garage doors of suburban houses. In the coun-tryside, many white farmers use two-way radios to operate their own rapid-response networks against stock-thieves and burglars.

Many white South Africans regard violent crime as being essentially an activity carried out by certain of their black compatriots, and fear of crime is used by white-led opposition parties and white journalists as a euphemism for fear of black rule, the traditional white South African fear of blacks *('swart gevaar')* in a new guise. Black township-dwellers, who in fact are more likely to suffer from crime than people living in suburbs, often blame the upsurge in crime on immigrants from elsewhere in Africa, who have flocked to the country since the opening of its borders in 1990. The South African Police Service, demoralized and ill-adapted to deal with the transition from apartheid to democracy, often appears overwhelmed. Police spokesmen admit that elements of the force have themselves been penetrated by organ-ized crime. Police commanders are acutely aware of the new interna-tional dimension to organized crime, particularly in regard to the drug trade, which has increased dramatically in recent years and has prompted the government to appeal for help to the US authorities. It is a fact that South Africa has become the target of major international criminal syndicates, notably from Nigeria, but also from as far afield as Russia and China. South Africa is a leading producer of marijuana and in just a few years has become a leading importer and re-exporter of cocaine and heroin,[1] as well as an attractive location for money-laundering and sophisticated business fraud. South Africa, in fact, has become Africa's capital of organized crime, with a total criminal turnover reckoned at some R.41.1 billion per year (Johnson, 1996). Criminals from abroad are attracted by the existence of a market for drugs and fraud, but equally important is the country's first-class

[1] 'South Africa: Drugs – Mandela's new struggle', *The Geopolitical Drug Dispatch*, No. 54 (April 1996), pp. 1–3.

transport infrastructure and banking system and the world's tenth-biggest stock exchange, which make it an ideal base for intercontinental operations and money-laundering.

The crime wave is particularly disappointing to the considerable number of people who assumed that violence generally would decline in South Africa after the abolition of apartheid. To be sure, the variant of national socialism introduced in 1948 in the form of apartheid had a profoundly destabilizing effect on South African society, including in the form of crime, and no serious observer believed that its effects would cease the instant a democratic government was installed. But what has become clearer since the election of an ANC government in 1994 is that crime in South Africa is not only, and perhaps not even primarily, the result of poverty. It is a social and even a political artifact.

The national security and intelligence services, and particularly the South African Police Service, are themselves part of the problem. For decades, the police concentrated so single-mindedly on the threat of communist subversion that it ignored the deep changes taking place in the political economy of crime in southern Africa and indeed worldwide. Far from concentrating their resources on combating crime, the police sometimes regarded important criminal syndicates as allies in the fight against the ANC and its partner and *alter ego*, the South African Communist Party (SACP). For as long as the country existed in its Cold War deep-freeze, it was relatively insulated against major international trends such as the narcotics trade. The normalization of foreign relations after 1990 opened the country to a flood of fortune-seekers from elsewhere, including some sophisticated criminal syndicates which were far more knowledgeable about the techniques of international crime than the country's law enforcement agencies. Boycotted by much of the international community, isolated from many conferences and exchanges, excluded from Interpol, the South African Police did not even have a unit to combat organized crime until 1993. By mid-1996, South Africa still had no laws against money-laundering.

Revolution, crime and security

That South Africa was indeed at war between the early 1960s and the early 1990s, and not merely undergoing particularly acute political difficulties, cannot be doubted.[2] During this period leaders of the ANC

[2] Some observers regard the Sharpeville massacre of 1960 as the true beginning of the war. The South African Communist Party and the African National Congress, both of which had been banned by law, formed an armed wing, Umkhonto we Sizwe, which issued a formal declaration of war on 16 December 1961. On 27 April 1994, South Africa's first general election resulted in the election of a government with a majority from the ANC.

and the SACP, the most important organizations of armed opposition, based in exile, explicitly regarded their struggle as revolutionary in nature, comparable to similar campaigns in Algeria, Vietnam and elsewhere. By and large the ANC and SACP were prevented by the effectiveness of police measures from undertaking substantial activity in South Africa between 1964 and the early 1980s, but their intention was plain. South Africa's white government, particularly after the mid-1970s, interpreted this revolutionary war as the spearhead of a 'total onslaught' – in the words of a 1977 Defence White Paper – orchestrated by the Soviet Union, which provided military, diplomatic and other support to the ANC and the SACP and to allied governments in Angola and Mozambique. South African army and police officers who had studied the theory and practice of revolutionary warfare, and who became known as 'securocrats' because of their belief that security structures could be used as a basis for managing political change, devised a counter-insurgency doctrine aimed at mobilizing every branch of the state in a campaign to defeat the total onslaught which they believed to be directed from Moscow. Murder, smuggling, forgery, propaganda and subversion were instruments used by both sides in the struggle, but it was the state which brought the greatest resources to bear in these domains.

Like many modern wars, it was less about locating and destroying the enemies' armed forces than about inducing the bulk of the population to accept a given political dispensation whose legitimacy could be accepted by international observers. It was, according to the securocrats, a struggle which was 80 per cent political and only 20 per cent military. Only in Angola between 1975 and 1989 did the war for control of South Africa take the form of conventional battles between rival armies. Strategists within both the South African Defence Force (SADF) and the ANC–SACP guerrilla army, Umkhonto we Sizwe, realized at an early stage that the outcome of the struggle would depend largely on achieving hegemony in local communities. This would be accomplished by constructing a political clientele among diverse social groups, particularly in the townships where the majority of South Africa's black urban population live and which both sides recognized as the key site of the struggle. From the mid-1980s the two principal state security forces, the South African Police and the SADF, adopted a strategy of systematically arming various social groups for use as auxiliaries, often called 'vigilantes', who would combat ANC supporters in society at large (Haysom, 1986). State-sanctioned vigilantes of this sort came from sections of the population opposed to the young comrades acting in the name of the ANC, and included established criminal gangs as well as individual convicts released from prison for the purpose. In 1986 the SADF secretly and illegally trained some 200 members of the Inkatha organization, the forerunner of the Inkatha Freedom Party, in counter-insurgency warfare. This decision was made by the government's supreme security organ, the State Security Council chaired by State President P.W. Botha, and these 200 later formed the nucleus of Inkatha's own private army. Violence in KwaZulu-Natal increased measurably in 1987 when the 200 trainees were thrown into the struggle against the ANC and SACP. There can be no doubt that the state itself fanned the flames of war in the province.

The policy of arming vigilantes was itself a reaction to the strategy of the ANC and SACP, who were smuggling guns into the townships and urging South Africans to make the country 'ungovernable' by refusing to pay rents and service charges and by murdering policemen, municipal councillors, suspected police informers and anyone else whom ANC sympathizers regarded as collaborators with the government. It was in 1985, during the explosion of popular anti-state violence which had started the previous year, that the method of lynching known as 'neck-lacing' was invented, a particularly terrifying form of execution since it was not only agonizingly painful, but also believed by many South Africans to destroy the soul as well as the body of the victim, preventing them from becoming an ancestor. The ANC and SACP urged on the lynch-mobs and only belatedly, and somewhat unconvincingly, condemned the use of the necklace. At the same time the most thoughtful ANC and SACP strategists were surprised and concerned by the resourcefulness and ruthlessness of the security forces when they began organizing popular counter-revolutionary violence to combat that encouraged by the ANC. Joe Slovo, for many years the chief of staff of Umkhonto we Sizwe, admitted ruefully to having underestimated 'the fact that the counter-revolution learns from the revolution' (Slovo, 1986: 25). Indeed, this was so. The SADF's approach was to study the techniques of guerrilla warfare used in Malaya, Algeria, Vietnam and other classic cases, and to employ the same techniques on behalf of the state with a view to throwing the insurrectionary campaign into reverse. 'The solution to the problem of defeating revolutionary warfare', asserted one author much studied by the securocrats in South Africa, ' is the application of its strategy and principles in reverse' (McCuen, 1966: 77).

The strategy elaborated by the ANC and SACP in 1978–9, after a study-tour by a group of leaders to Vietnam, envisaged a combination of political and military activity. In the first phase military activity would take the form of 'armed propaganda', the execution of military activities designed less to destroy the enemy's capacity to make war than to advertise to the people of South Africa the presence of Umkhonto we Sizwe and its ability to strike. Among the best-known examples of such activities carried out in the phase of 'armed propaganda' were the sabotage of oil installations at Sasolburg in 1980, a rocket attack on the military base at Voortrekkerhoogte in 1981, and the planting of a car bomb outside Air Force headquarters in the heart of Pretoria in May 1983. These were highly effective in boosting the ANC's standing among radicals. The intention of the High Command of Umkhonto we Sizwe was eventually to proceed to the next stage of the struggle which they called 'people's war', a generalized, revolutionary uprising in which trained guerrillas would play a strategic role, but in which most of the activities would be carried out with a high degree of spontaneity by ordinary civilians.

It was in this light that the ANC and SACP interpreted the outbreak of a popular uprising which began in the Vaal Triangle area in 1984 and soon spread to other parts of South Africa. Like the earlier insurrection in Soweto in 1976, the 1984 rising arose from an essentially local cycle of violent incidents and repression. It was not organized by any specific group. The ANC, believing that the last phase of struggle, 'people's war', was now close at hand, welcomed the rising and aimed to stoke the fires of revolution by propaganda, by developing its political connections inside the country, and by infiltrating guns and trained guerrillas into the townships. Although the uprising was not organized by the ANC, and nor were the leaders of popular militancy in regular contact with ANC headquarters in Lusaka, the presence of ANC guerrillas and the spreading of ANC slogans and propaganda served to legitimize a wide variety of acts of violence in the eyes of young radicals especially and to convince the comrades that their actions were indeed political ones.

The fact that the ANC explicitly encouraged the spread of popular violence during the 1980s has caused some commentators to argue that its call to render the country ungovernable was the main cause of the culture of violence and lawlessness which has become widespread among South African youth in particular (Kane-Berman, 1993). It was undoubtedly a contributing factor, and it is ironic inasmuch as the ANC today is responsible for a problem which is at least in part of its own making. However, it is both one-sided and superficial to attach the main responsibility for the spread of a popular culture of violence to the ANC, the SACP or any other anti-apartheid organization. In the first place, the South African townships had a long history of violence occasionally taking the form of local uprisings, even as far back as the 1940s. The main cause of this no doubt lay in the very fabric of modern South African history, in the destruction of the black peasantry and rapid and chaotic urbanization. Moreover, the state itself could be said to have precipitated violence by banning certain political parties including the SACP in 1950 and the ANC in 1960, at a time when neither of these organizations had adopted a policy of armed struggle. The Sharpeville massacre was perpetrated by the police in 1960, over a year before the ANC's own turn to violence. However, once the armed propaganda of Umkhonto we Sizwe had started to become effective in the early 1980s, and once the ANC and SACP had endorsed the strategy of making South Africa 'ungovernable', spontaneous popular violence in a variety of forms became a political act. The fact that this was countered by the government's arming of counter-revolutionary elements meant that, in effect, both the ANC and the security forces were competing for years to turn many of the country's black communities into armed camps. This they did in order to tip the national balance of power in their favour. The crime and the popular violence which are rooted in South Africa's long history of conquest and shorter experience of industrialization, and in the apartheid system by which it was governed, were also given a political complexion as a result of decisions taken by specific political actors.

Politics and crime in South Africa: a brief history

The agency of the state responsible for combating crime in South Africa is the police force founded in 1913, which played such a leading role in the long struggle against the ANC and the SACP.

Throughout its history, the South African Police – to use its former name – has had a semi-military nature. Long before the outbreak of hostilities in the 1960s, and indeed even before the National Party government came to power in 1948, the South African Police had developed a specific view of how to police African populations. The origins of this lie in the British colonial tradition of indirect rule. As practised throughout British colonies in Africa, indirect rule was based on the aim of keeping Africans as far as possible in rural areas under their own traditional or quasi-traditional rulers. In South Africa, where the mining economy required large amounts of cheap labour, exceptions were made to allow rural African men in particular to move to the towns as migrants who would come to live in cities and mine-compounds for a specific period before returning to their home areas and their families after their contracts had expired. They were discouraged from settling permanently in urban areas and from developing political institutions there. The key to indirect rule was for government officials to identify and promote local rulers, hereditary chiefs if possible, who would govern the rural areas as far as possible by their own devices and according to customary law. The role of the national police force was to ensure that chiefs did not contravene the laws of the central government which applied in those rural areas designated as African reserves, or the later apartheid creations of bantustans or homelands, and to act as a mobile armed force when intervention was necessary. Any significant agitation against a chief regarded by the government as legitimate was interpreted by the police as a form of insurgency, and when, in the 1950s, there were several major cases of rural disturbance in South Africa arising from protests against the stringent apartheid laws then being introduced, and to some extent articulated by nationalist movements such as the ANC and, later, the Pan-Africanist Congress (PAC), this was perceived by police chiefs as a form of crime. Indeed, after the banning of the ANC and the PAC in 1960, mere membership of these organizations was a crime, as membership of the SACP had been since 1950.

The formal outbreak of guerrilla war in South Africa in 1961 took the form of an urban sabotage campaign organized by an underground ANC and SACP leadership based in the cities. This was comprehensively defeated by the police in 1963–4. Thereafter, while the PAC remained ineffective, the ANC and the SACP, based in exile in Tanzania and, later, Zambia, turned to a new strategy, called 'hacking the way home'. It envisaged a campaign of rural guerrilla warfare, beginning with campaigns in Rhodesia in 1967–8, intended ultimately to open up a Ho Chi Minh trail to South Africa. South African Police units were sent to Rhodesia to work alongside the Rhodesian security forces to counter this threat. At the same time a further theatre of rural conflict opened up in the north of Namibia, the South African colony threatened by the guerrilla army of the South-West African People's Organization (SWAPO), based first in Zambia and, after 1975, in newly independent Angola. In keeping with the old colonial tradition, South African policemen regarded these major incidents of armed insurgency as a particularly serious form of crime rather than as a political matter or a war in the conventional sense (Cawthra, 1993: 14–19).

It is notable that it was the South African Police and not the SADF which was deployed in Rhodesia and, initially, in Namibia. Officers from the Security Branch of the police who had worked in Rhodesia later established a special counter-insurgency unit in Namibia, Koevoet, which was to have a considerable influence on South Africa itself. The main function of Koevoet was the identification and elimination of suspected insurgents, contrary to the main principle of policing, which is to detect, arrest and prosecute wrong-doers in conformity with the law, using minimum force. Its officers were preoccupied with kill-ratios and body-counts. Particularly alarming, from the point of view of traditional policing, was the practice developed by Koevoet of inducing captured guerrillas to work for the security forces, a process known as 'turning'. They were then used as troopers in the security forces without even being given a formal indemnity for their earlier offences. In the long run this could only bring the central principle of the law into disrepute. 'Turned' guerrillas, known as *askaris*, made particularly fearsome killers. Battle-hardened, they were psychologically and socially divorced from their communities of origin, rather like the slave armies of history. Former Koevoet officers were later to form special death-squads organized by the South African Police, largely composed of 'turned' former guerrillas from SWAPO, the ANC, the PAC and several defunct guerrilla armies of southern Africa. Some Koevoet officers, such as Colonel Eugene de Kock, commander of the C-1 unit of the South African Police, the leading police death-squad, became deeply involved in weapons smuggling and other forms of serious crime, both as police officers and on their own account. One of De Kock's most faithful lieutenants, an Angolan, had actually been trained in China in the 1960s, embarking on a revolutionary path which eventually led him to membership of an apartheid death-squad.

The techniques of counter-insurgency developed by the South African Police in Rhodesia and Namibia soon made their appearance in urban areas. Colonel Theunis 'Rooi Rus' Swanepoel, the architect of the bloody repression of the Soweto rising of 1976, for example, had taken part in the first counter-insurgency operations against SWAPO in northern Namibia ten years earlier (*ibid.:* 19). By 1975 there were over 2,000 South African policemen serving in Rhodesia, and they brought their experience to bear on the home front. Tactics learned in the border wars in Rhodesia and Namibia, including techniques of disinformation, pseudo-operations and the use of 'turned' captives, gradually made their appearance in urban areas of South Africa. To this was added a growing ruthlessness in the use of torture and sweeping legal powers, as well as other techniques learned from other countries including Israel, Chile and Argentina, the latter at the height of 'dirty wars' of their own (*ibid*: 19, 27).

The absence of any political strategy or even full administrative recognition in regard to black urban areas until as late as the 1980s put the police in a difficult position. At best, they were expected to enforce apartheid laws which, like the Pass Laws and the Group Areas Act, became steadily more unworkable as the police were overwhelmed by the sheer numbers of people living in illegal situations. Since the government itself insisted, in the face of all evidence to the contrary, that black people were living only temporarily in the cities, it was not possible for them to develop sensitive approaches to policing black urban areas or techniques which relied on the essential element of all successful policing, namely the co-operation of the public itself. In keeping with the traditions of indirect rule, according to which the politics of quasi-traditional chieftaincies were the only legitimate political arena for black communities, they continued to regard all forms of nationalist activity, or even of protest about living conditions, as tantamount to crime. At the same time they made relatively little effort to prevent or prosecute everyday forms of crime in black townships, tending to concentrate ordinary domestic policing in white South African areas, intervening in the townships only inadequately or when crime threatened to take on a recognizably political form, such as if people perceived as troublemakers threatened to make common cause with banned or suspect organizations such as the SACP or the ANC. The lack of an effective strategy for policing black urban areas was compounded by the lawlessness produced by rapid urbanization, which bred crime of a conventional type in the form of criminal gangs specializing in racketeering, rape and theft.

The old colonial tradition of indirect rule combined with the exigencies of policing rapidly growing and poorly administered black urban areas to produce a constant search for individuals or social groups who could help the police with their most basic functions of information-gathering and, as the years went by, identifying and arresting nationalist agitators. The police, drawing on their rural experience, continued in an urban environment their search for local strong men who could govern the particular ethnic units into which, according to their analysis, black South African society was divided. Since there were no hereditary chiefs with authority in the townships, the search sometimes encompassed informal associations or even criminal gangs, particularly when these were composed of rural migrants with conservative honour-codes and strong roots in the countryside, who despised the indiscipline of the township youths whom they equated with criminals or *tsotsis* (Bonner, 1993). Such groups, like the famous gang called the Russians which flourished in the 1950s in townships on the Reef, sometimes appeared to the police to be stabilizing elements in a chaotic social milieu. Even in the 1950s the police sometimes tolerated such groups and permitted them to set up quite extensive systems of control, with their own system of kangaroo courts (Freed, 1963: 78, 116).

If the South African government continued to regard black Africans as posing the greatest problem to the security of state and society when they moved to towns where they risked becoming politicized by nationalist organizations, the ANC and SACP themselves came to a broadly similar conclusion. After their unsuccessful foray into semi-conventional rural guerrilla warfare in Rhodesia in 1967–8, they decided that the struggle for South Africa was overwhelmingly urban in nature. Influenced by the SACP's classic Marxist-Leninist approach, South Africa's premier anti-apartheid organization concentrated its efforts on mobilizing the urban working class in the struggle. Like their opposite numbers the securocrats, the ANC and SACP leaders saw political and military activity as a seamless web. And so, when the government belatedly began to recognize the reality of black urban life, and encouraged the creation of local political structures there, the populations of the largest black townships became the site of a struggle for control between the state's attempt to set up black town councils which would provide the black urban areas with self-government, and informal social groups whom the ANC encouraged to take a revolutionary path, themselves countered in turn by government-sponsored vigilantes.

From the mid-1980s until as late as 1994, both the security forces and the ANC–SACP were arming their supporters in the townships in pursuit of this strategy. This is the provenance of many of the weapons used by South African criminals today.

Narratives of violence, local and national

During the wave of popular insurrections which began in 1984, the network of pro-ANC activists called the United Democratic Front (UDF) was remarkably successful in persuading people from different sections of society, living in a wide variety of situations, that their local or particular grievances were ultimately caused by the existence of apartheid. The variety of social groups eventually included in the broad front represented by the UDF was diverse in the extreme: Christian activists and liberal intellectuals, trade unionists, unemployed youth, township thugs and Marxist revolutionaries, but also rural youth mobilized against chiefs and even against witches (Van Kessel, 1995). People from all of these groups operated under the banner of the UDF, itself loosely affiliated with the ANC leadership in exile with which it was forbidden by law to communicate openly. So successful was the popular front led by the UDF that the National Party government and its security chiefs eventually came to the conclusion that the state could not withstand resistance on such a scale indefinitely, even if the security forces were able to prevent its physical overthrow. Once the leaders of the National Party had drawn this conclusion, the unbanning of the ANC was a logical consequence. While the negotiations which began officially in 1990 and the elections of 1994 helped to eliminate political violence at the national level, they made far less impact on the many local struggles which underlay the national contest, which continue to follow a logic of their own to this day in a very different national and international context (du Toit, 1993).

Complex social struggles which are rooted in local communities, particularly when they have been militarized by the action of armed revolutionaries and state security officers, do not end when the formal organizations contesting state power declare an end to hostilities. Thus, many of the social groups which participated in the struggle for South Africa continue to pursue their factional interests by violence. Today, this is generally labelled as criminal rather than political violence, but the change of vocabulary should not blind us to the fact that the actors remain largely the same. Whereas the UDF was so successful in persuading many South Africans that apartheid was the root cause of their various factional or local grievances, the change in the political landscape since 1994 has made this rallying call obsolete, leaving the ANC government bereft of a political message which can unite the dispossessed of South Africa and crusaders for justice as the revolutionary slogans once did.

Just as it is ironic that the ANC must now deal with the violence which it once encouraged, so the security forces now have to struggle against forms of violence which they originally organized in the shape of former allies or auxiliaries who have access to firearms originally procured for them by Military Intelligence or other organs of the state. Some former guerrillas who are unable to find work have become professional criminals or have joined the numerous informal militias which have sprouted throughout the country with only tenuous links to political parties. Whether or not they adopt political labels, local gangs or militias all too often provide a living for young men who have few other prospects of finding a job: there is a thin dividing line between the gangsters who operate protection rackets within their territories and the militias which raise taxes from every household in their area on the grounds that this is necessary to pay for community self-defence. Local militias which develop links with whichever political party governs their area may derive further benefits in the form of protection from prosecution and access to some of the spoils of public office, such as jobs or, for local businessmen, licences to run bottle stores and taxi companies. The feuds between rival taxi operators, which sometimes give rise to deadly gun battles, are closely linked to local politics in this way. In some areas, particularly of KwaZulu-Natal, control of a taxi firm not only brings profits but enables a local militia boss to regulate the weapons and marijuana trades locally and to supervise population movements in his area. It is in KwaZulu-Natal that violent competition between local militias continues on the greatest scale and is so clearly connected to national political rivalries as to constitute a low-level civil war.

Political clienteles, we may reflect, are built not only by the distribution of patronage, but also by coercion and persuasion. At the beginning of the war in the early 1960s the government controlled most systems of patronage and had an effective monopoly of legitimate violence. As the years went by, and it progressively lost control of these instruments and found itself losing the propaganda war as well, the government's response was to increase its use of coercion. As we have seen, this was done not only by the increasingly ruthless methods of the security forces themselves, culminating in the formation of official death-squads, but also by arming certain groups in the black population, which served the purpose of simultaneously making war on ANC sympathizers and helping form new clusters of political allies among the black population at minimum risk to white lives. The creation of ethnic militias was a technique learned by police officers with counter-insurgency experience in Rhodesia and Namibia, as well as by military men who had learned from Portuguese experience in southern Africa and from other colonial wars. The most successful such attempt at forming an ethnic 'contra' force was in regard to Inkatha, whose support was solidly rooted in the rural areas of Zululand.

Before 1990, while the police could not entirely prevent revolutionary organizations from disseminating propaganda, it could largely prevent them from building a formal base. After the unbanning of these organizations in 1990 this too became an impossible task. Since the ANC's election victory of 1994, local ANC branches have had access to some of the resources of government, enabling local party chieftains to build a real patronage network to buttress their power. In KwaZulu-Natal, this is contested by Inkatha Freedom Party bosses who aspire to do the same, using the resources of the only province which the IFP governs. The police, having lost their ability to crush such networks and being now under the tutelage of an ANC minister, watch nervously. Much depends on the personality and resourcefulness of the local police commander, who has to become something of a diplomat in order to keep peace in his area.

The security forces are not, and never have been, impartial as far as most black South Africans are concerned. Not only has history left a legacy of distrust between the police and supporters of black-dominated political parties, but some explicitly criminal gangs have developed close relations with the security forces. This has produced within some sections of the security forces a highly ambiguous attitude towards certain types of crime. During the last phase of the guerrilla war some police and army officers even developed criminal enterprises of their own, such as in the weapons, gems, ivory and marijuana trades, partly for their own profit and partly as a covert means of providing arms and funds for informal militias opposed to the ANC and the SACP. The range of state-sanctioned law-breaking included sophisticated smuggling operations and currency frauds which brought the government's own secret services into business relationships with major smuggling syndicates, Italian Mafia money-launderers and other operators in the international criminal underworld (Ellis, 1996a). Even the august South African Reserve Bank turned a blind eye to currency fraud committed on behalf of the state (Potgieter, 1995: 147–9). It was in this culture that the so-called Third Force arose, a network of security officials who organized violence, both with and without the formal approval of government ministers, in an effort to alter the balance of power in negotiations between the National Party and the ANC between 1990 and 1994. This further complicates the relations between political parties, party-aligned militias, criminal gangs and the police at the local level today.

Cross-border conflict and trade

The war for control of South Africa was also fought abroad, especially in Mozambique and Angola. Whereas the ANC and the SACP, the PAC and others attempted to establish guerrilla bases in neighbouring countries within striking distance of South Africa, the South African security forces attempted to counter them by direct attack, by destabilizing (Hanlon, 1986) neighbouring states and by using networks of professional smugglers as sources of intelligence and instruments of subversion. It was the strategy of destabilizing neighbouring states which first brought South African intelligence officers into complicity with the smuggling networks which, from the 1970s onwards, were an increasingly important resource in the political economy of the region (Ellis, 1994). At the same time, the application of international sanctions against South Africa caused a variety of government departments to become engaged in the international smuggling of major goods and commodities, including oil and weapons. As South African intelligence officers became smugglers and money-launderers, some individuals developed criminal relationships for purely personal enrichment, and some such liaisons have survived the change of government in 1994. Intelligence officers ordered or encouraged to smuggle and defraud in the name of national security found it progressively easier and more tempting to do this on their own account as they saw the power of the National Party inexorably slipping away and as they began to think hard about their own financial future and that of their families after apartheid. Corruption in the public service increased rapidly as a result of the 'total strategy' of counter-revolution. Since the early 1990s, considerable numbers of those very counter-insurgency officers who developed close connections with professional criminals in the course of their work have left government service to work in the private sector. Many have become conventional businessmen, farmers or administrators or work for private security firms. Some at least combine legitimate enterprises with management of prostitution and arms-trafficking both locally and internationally. It appears that a handful have established interests in the new narcotics trade.

Some of the toughest of the elite troops of the former SADF work for a security company called Executive Outcomes Ltd which has negotiated major contracts for security work with governments in Angola, Sierra Leone and elsewhere. The directors and managers of Executive Outcomes enjoy the active support of some senior members of the erstwhile enemy organization, the ANC, and wield considerable influence in other parts of Africa; at one time they virtually kept the government of Sierra Leone in power, for example. Executive Outcomes is far more than a group of mercenaries. A legitimate company, it employs intelligence analysts and technical staff, and by 1995 had generated over 30 subsidiary companies throughout sub-Saharan Africa specializing in activities including air transport, video production and mining. It has contracts in East Africa, the Indian Ocean and the Middle East. Several of Executive Outcomes' senior personnel previously worked for a South African Special Forces' death-squad known as the Civil Co-operation Bureau. Other companies which began life in the service of the counter-insurgency strategy of the South African state also continue in business, such as GMR (Pty) Ltd, a company set up by an Italian businessman in the Seychelles and now run by a former naval officer who served as a private secretary of President P.W. Botha. GMR sold arms to the Rwandan government in the months prior to the 1994 genocide in Rwanda and continues to trade with the UNITA organization in Angola (Ellis, 1996a: 170–8).

In short, certain types of illicit activity in South Africa are linked to international trading networks both legal and illegal through the activities of sophisticated operators who have access to large amounts of capital. Some of these operators have high-level connections in politics and the security forces, and they are able to broker transactions between powerful factions inside South Africa and abroad. Particularly important in this respect is Mozambique, whose own state infrastructure was largely eroded during a long war in which the SADF played an important role. Mozambique today has effectively become a free trade area for businessmen and smugglers of every description. Since the country produces little for export and has only a small domestic market, it is essentially an entrepôt for onward trade. Especially significant are those former South African military intelligence operatives who have influence with Mozambican politicians and officials and who are able to use Mozambique as a centre for offshore transactions involving South Africa itself.

The political economy of crime

Crime in South Africa is rooted in the country's history, including that of apartheid. The particular forms it takes have been shaped by the war against apartheid at a number of levels. At the local level, particularly in poor black communities, armed militias or gangs attempt to control territory from which they derive economic benefits. Some reach an understanding with local police officers who are unable to enforce the law fully and who may in any case have developed alliances with various unofficial armed groups over many years. Some such groups develop vertical alliances with national political parties or individual politicians and with businessmen who can import the goods which they most require – guns – and who will buy the goods which they offer for export, notably marijuana and stolen cars.

Some middlemen have good connections in politics and the security services, especially those who are themselves veterans of the covert actions of the past. During the cross-border struggle between the South African security forces and the ANC, SACP, PAC and SWAPO, armed groups of all types sprang up throughout southern Africa, and many of the security and intelligence forces of the region have been penetrated by criminal groups in a complex network of relationships. Senior politicians and intelligence officers in Mozambique are widely regarded as having interests in smuggling concerns including the drug trade. The same is true of Zambia, Angola, the Seychelles and elsewhere.

The countries of southern Africa are closely linked in an economic system constructed by the British government and the great mining houses in the late nineteenth and early twentieth centuries, with only Angola, of all the countries in the region, standing largely outside this highly integrated trading system. As the outlying parts of the southern African economic system have grown poorer, not least as a result of the war for control of South Africa which brought about such destruction, so their formal economies have shrunk to be replaced by informal economies and cross-border trades which are technically illicit, but whose existence is widely known. While South Africa remains at the hub of the region's formal economy, it also stands at the centre of this burgeoning smuggling economy. It is not only in Mozambique, Angola and Zambia that senior figures in government and the formal economy sometimes play a key role in the smuggling economy as well, but also in South Africa. It was South African military intelligence officers who succeeded in establishing Johannesburg as the hub of the ivory and rhino horn trades from the late 1970s, with the personal approval of General Malan, then head of the SADF and later Minister of Defence (Kumleben, 1996). According to the head of the Organized Crime Unit of the South African Police Services, the leading gold smugglers are often rich businessmen seeking to export capital in contravention of the currency laws.[3] South African mines are estimated to lose some 1.5 billion rands' worth of gold per year to theft, and gold smugglers export this by air or sea to neighbouring countries and thence to Europe. The diamond marketing cartel, De Beers, has traditionally had an intimate acquaintance with the gem-smuggling trade because of its concern to purchase stones which are unofficially mined and marketed as well as the official production of various countries.

South Africa attracts criminals from abroad not only because it constitutes a substantial market for drugs and fraud, but also because it is an ideal base for operations elsewhere. At the same time, its relative prosperity attracts millions of people from countries to the north who are not professional criminals, but are simply desperate to earn a living. Here the economic failure of other parts of Africa shapes South Africa's own underground economy. For example, traders from Zambia and the Democratic Republic of Congo seeking to buy consumer goods in South Africa for resale at home often have no access to a suitable form of cash, since the currencies of Congo and Zambia have no international value. They sometimes acquire small quantities of gems, gold, ivory, rhino horn, local works of art or any other goods which are easily transportable and which they take to South Africa as a form of currency rather than as a commodity. In a highly organized trade, cars stolen in South Africa are often exported via Mozambique to points further north as far as Nairobi as a form of easily transportable wealth for the settlement of payments agreed particularly in the course of drug transactions, although they have also been traced as far afield as Turkey and New Zealand.

The growth of a regional economy of crime from the 1970s, and later of social movements which contested incumbent governments throughout southern Africa in various forms from religious revivals to campaigns in favour of democracy, was misinterpreted by South African security officers who overestimated the degree to which political and social disturbances throughout the region were due to Soviet aggression. And, while the Soviet Union did indeed acquire, via the SACP, very considerable influence over the ANC, the latter never achieved real control of the array of social forces inside South Africa which it claimed as its supporters. Meanwhile the very relentlessness of the securocrats' reaction helped to confirm the popular belief that apartheid itself was the source of all social problems. The government was prepared to murder people like Steve Biko and many others who were not communists or agents of Moscow and had not taken up arms

---

[3] 'Surge in gold smuggling robs mines and economy', *Business Day*, 9 May 1996.

in opposition to the government, but were simply unofficial spokes-men for substantial sections of black society or, in other words, were politicians. Their murder made them into martyrs and narrowed still further the political ground which the National Party government hoped to contest. The fact that these murders were perpetrated by the government's own security forces jeopardized the ability of the organs of public safety and public protection to uphold the law in future.

Throughout the 1980s the South African government ignored or underestimated some of the key changes taking place in the world, pre-ferring to see everything through a Cold War prism. In fact, politics and economies throughout southern Africa, and many other parts of the world as well, were becoming less formal and less state-dominated as a result of profound changes in international relations. Within South Africa the extra-parliamentary politics of the 1980s represented civic action by a vast array of social groups motivated by a wide range of grievances. These the state continued to regard as illegitimate and even communist-inspired. The securocrats were aware of the political nature of their struggle but, being overwhelmingly military men, were inca-pable of analysing politics other than as top-down systems of com-mand, patronage and coercion. The National Party itself remained shackled to the white electorate which had brought it to power and sus-tained it for decades, and when it did finally turn itself into a non-racial organization after 1990, the change was too late to make much impact.

Just as not all threats to the South African state in fact stemmed from Soviet activity, as the government asserted, so, too, apartheid was not the unique cause of evil. The social changes which helped to pro-duce illegitimate violence and crime generally were also the conse-quences of larger changes which are fairly typical of industrializing countries in general. These include the decline of the rural economy and of the peasantry, the disruption of family and social life associated with labour migration, and the decline of older systems of moral econ-omy. South African society has for decades, even before apartheid, been prey to a high incidence of social problems expressed, among other ways, in the form of broken families, domestic violence, and criminal violence without any form of political intent, particularly in urban areas.

In a healthy multi-party political system such as South Africa aspires to today, it is necessary for social grievances to find non-vio-lent forms of expression both within and outside the political field. Here it is worth mentioning the curious transformation of the ANC itself. Because of its banning in 1960, the ANC did not develop at a crucial period of its history as a conventional political party as it might reasonably have been expected to do. Under apartheid it became the legitimizing element for all manner of social struggles whose actual organizational forms were those of civil society unable to find proper political expression. There can be no doubt of the ANC's deep popularity among South Africans, but one effect of its becoming a party of government has been to call into question the nature of its relationship as a political organization with South African society more generally. It is noticeable that some of the great dynamism of South African social movements, notably those enlisted in the struggle against apartheid in the 1980s, has evaporated since the ANC entered government, not because the fundamental problems of South African society have disappeared, but because the most talented organizers of social movements have now taken on public office and become administrators of the public good rather than militants for social justice. It remains to be seen to what extent the ANC in government can remain attentive to the social causes which it championed when it was an umbrella for social opposition to apartheid. Conversely, it remains to be seen to what extent South Africa has indeed become ungovernable by any government at all, at least temporarily, and whether citizens are able to redress their grievances by means of social and political action through the range of legal institutions which now exists.

The international context is now quite different from that of the 1980s, and the transformation has been accentuated by South Africa's emergence from international isolation into a world in rapid mutation. In much of Africa formal political institutions and formal economies have declined in importance, as powerful factions and individuals increasingly make use of informal economies and the informal political alliances which produce 'shadow states',[4] patterns of politics and economics at variance with the official and formal structures which, in theory, exist to articulate these fundamental human activities. Since the abolition of apartheid, South Africa is more than ever before tied to the region in which it is located. Quite apart from the domestic factors which tend to weaken the state's monopoly of legitimate violence and which encourage the development of a criminal economy, the country cannot stand apart from the trends which are in evidence elsewhere. Some criminal trades, such as those in drugs (increasing rapidly), and in illegal weapons, are international in nature. Large amounts of money are generated by these trades and some of the profits are likely to be recycled in the form of political finance by criminal bosses in search of political cover.

Southern Africa is not the only part of the world where politics and crime have become closely associated and South Africa is not the only state which, in its struggle to mobilize all possible means and all available social forces for its own preservation, has condoned the creation

---

[4] On 'shadow states', see Reno, 1995; for a general view, see Ellis, 1996b.

of criminal enterprises by its own intelligence officers. The great majority of South African police officers and politicians are deeply concerned about the incidence of crime and its penetration of the state, and they can at least count themselves fortunate that the process has proceeded less far than in some other countries. The formation of new power blocs by professional criminals, secret service officers and senior officials working together has not claimed control of the state itself to the same degree as in Russia, for example (Waller and Yasmann, 1995). Nor have South African politicians combined tenure of public office with personal enrichment to anything approaching the extent in some other important African countries, such as Nigeria and former Zaïre.

In practice, probably the most pressing question for South Africa is to ascertain whether it is possible for criminal activity to be success-fully contained in such a way as to permit the functioning of a con-ventional political and economic sector, with all that that implies with regard to the rule of law and the security of individuals. Private secu-rity guards and fortified suburbs have no doubt become permanent features of South African life, just as in many other parts of the world. In some parts of South Africa a form of warlordism may have become endemic for the foreseeable future, again like some other parts of the world. This does not necessarily imply the further erosion of the state or even of the conventional business sector, since warlordism does not exist in a separate world from official politics but has become an inte-gral part of the political system through the relations between party bosses and the actual perpetrators of illicit violence. The examples of Mexico, Italy and Colombia, to name but three, may well be of rele-vance to South Africa in showing how a highly developed system of criminal syndicates with connections to political parties and the secu-rity forces can co-exist with high rates of economic growth and con-ventional business activity.

4

The 'Social Capital' of the State as an Agent of Deception

or the Ruses of Economic Intelligence

BÉATRICE HIBOU

In the early 1980s, in the enthusiasm for universal liberal remedies fashionable at the time, a number of factors were considered to justify the application of structural adjustment programmes to African economies. These factors included the inability of African economies to adjust to the world economic crisis, their relative backwardness by comparison with other developing economies, their growing burden of debt, and a degree of corruption which was having an adverse effect on production. The aim of structural adjustment programmes was to restore the health of public finances as quickly as possible and then, step by step, to give some of the world's poorest economies a new start. Imposed by the main international financial institutions, the International Monetary Fund and the World Bank, and by foreign bilateral donors, the reforms generally contained a financial component including the re-establishment of balanced budgets, reform of fiscal systems, debt alleviation, and the restructuring and privatization of the banking system. They also included a commercial component, which involved the liberalization of domestic and foreign trade and the closure of marketing boards and some other regulatory bodies. A third aspect was economic reform, typically including a streamlining of the procedures governing production and investment and the privatization of publicly owned companies.

Faced with progress slower than expected, and in reaction to criticisms that structural adjustment programmes were not well adapted to African conditions, the architects of reform later introduced two new elements in most of their programmes. The first was a legislative package which included an overhaul of the labour market and a revision of employment and company law and the second a political-institutional element, generally aiming to reform the institutions of state ('capacity-building') and to improve the quality of governance. The reduction of corruption and of arbitrariness in matters of administration and the absorption of informal or parallel networks and markets into the formal economic sector were seen, reasonably enough, as objectives necessary for the smooth functioning of market economies.

Some two decades after the imposition of the first structural adjustment programme, the process of adjustment is bogged down, the debt problem remains unsolved, and the 1980s are unanimously considered to have been a lost decade for Africa. There is increasing talk of the scale of corruption, of smuggling, of criminalization, and of war and anarchy. This chapter aims to explain this apparently paradoxical development. In the course of doing so, we shall observe the ambivalence of the actions taken by aid donors in an effort to halt Africa's course towards disaster and the complexity of the strategies adopted by different actors in African economies. Struggles to derive individual or factional benefit from economic reforms, waged partly outside the legal sphere, and the privatization of the administration and of public affairs in general, are the main reasons why the social capital of African economies today takes the form of a widespread use of deception and a range of what have aptly been described as 'dirty tricks' (an expression taken from Migdal, 1988: chap. 6).

How African economies have absorbed reforms

The failure of structural adjustment in Africa is often attributed to the absence of 'ownership' of reforms by local actors. Because the reforms have been imposed from outside, so this theory goes, they have been only partially accepted and have been implemented half-heartedly, if at all. Economic reforms are perceived as having disturbed various local arrangements without succeeding in replacing them with more satisfactory ones. It is this line of thinking which has led the most important aid donors and financial institutions to broaden their interventions so as to encompass the fields of 'good governance' and institutional improvement. However, an examination of the actual consequences of structural adjustment, as opposed to a study of its intended benefits, reveals the extraordinarily high degree to which reform measures have been appropriated by African actors. Liberalization measures have been so effectively integrated into the political economy and the particular trajectory of African economies that they have reinforced the very tendencies which they were supposed to counter, including extra-legal developments and the appropriation of economic resources by certain actors for purposes connected with the political and social control of populations.

The economy of plunder and its forms

The term 'economy of plunder', inspired by Hoskins (1976), refers to the acquisition, by the representatives of public authority, of economic resources for private purposes. We may observe in Africa today that, contrary to the teachings of the neo-liberal rubric, measures of privatization and financial liberalization can lead to a plundering of the economy as widespread as did the processes of nationalization, and perhaps in an even less orderly manner.

The privatization of public enterprises: If public enterprises in Africa have recorded such mediocre results, it is almost exclusively due to the fact that they have been systematically plundered for purposes of enrichment and the accumulation of power by members of the elite. The methods used include the diversion of funds to private accounts, the failure to allocate resources to the designated target areas, the utilization of institutional resources for private gain, the utilization of an enterprise's borrowing capacity for improper purposes, the constitution of private clientelist networks through nepotism or the creation of unnecessary posts, and so on. In some countries this process appeared very rapidly because of the suddenness and the extent of nationalization, with former Zaïre being the classic example. The subsequent path taken by public sector and parastatal enterprises in such cases is well known and has been abundantly documented. This is the main reason why the main financial institutions have insisted on the privatization of such public companies as a condition for further aid.

However, a detailed analysis of the actual practice of privatization in Africa demonstrates the degree to which it fails to produce an efficient allocation of productive resources. Still less does it free former public enterprises from state intervention or make the economic sector independent from politics. It is commonplace to observe that privatization measures are frequently the occasions for the payment of kickbacks and a high degree of corruption generally, and for the systematic manipulation of the uncertainties which surround the institution being privatized. The criteria for evaluating tenders are rarely transparent and the revenue earned from the sale of a privatized enterprise is often far lower than the costs of its rehabilitation. Generally, it is difficult to establish an objectively correct market value for such an enterprise, and the costs of restructuring are often little known in advance, while the productivity of a company under privatization and the nature of relevant markets are also often inadequately understood, added to which is the fact that privatizations take place in a situation where the future course of the economy is more than usually uncertain. However, what can be said with confidence is that the future of African economies will unfold, like everything else, within the conventions governing Africa's social and political life, in other words those of the economy of plunder organized by the elites which enjoy power.

It would be incorrect to conclude from the above that the economy of plunder takes the form of the privatization of public enterprises alone, now that nationalization has run its course. Even if it is difficult to establish the precise number of privatizations which have taken place in Africa, all the available studies demonstrate that the procedure has been adopted with painful slowness, that governments are reluctant to privatize, and that there is an absence of credible purchasers. The number of privatizations which have been completed is very small compared to the number of enterprises earmarked for privatization, and those sales which have taken place have raised relatively small sums. The directors of the main public and parastatal enterprises invariably belong to the ruling circle, as in Côte d'Ivoire, where the Thiam brothers, nephews of the late President Houphouët-Boigny, have served as directors of the Société ivoirienne de raffinage, the Société des transports d'Abidjan, the Société ivoirienne des chemins de fer, and, recently, the former Direction de contrôle des grands travaux (DCGTx). In Cameroon, the Société nationale des hydrocarbures and the other main instruments for diverting or siphoning public funds are ever more tightly in the grip of members of the 'Beti lobby'.

It should be noted, however, that the privatization of the economy can be defined more widely than simply the cession of public enterprises to private actors. It can include the acquisition, the creation or the conquest of markets by various means by persons linked to those in power but operating in a private capacity. In this sense, the privatization of the economy today is truly massive and in effect is the main form taken by the economy of plunder.

In general, procedures for privatization are concentrated in the hands of those close to the head of state. However, to the extent that privatizations today represent one of the few means of accumulating wealth, they are the occasions for intense conflict between factions. The so-called 'war of the chiefs' *('guerre des chefs')* in the early 1990s in Côte d'Ivoire between Henri Konan Bedié and Alassane Ouattara, or current factional struggles in Cameroon, take place most obviously in struggles behind closed doors for control of the measures of privatization, with each player trying to enlist a clientele for himself and to acquire the resources necessary to finance the logistics of his political strategy and its attendant needs.

This is the main reason why the procedures and decision-making processes governing privatization measures are everywhere opaque in the extreme, and complex to the point of being unfathomable. At the heart of them, always, are the acolytes of those in power. Nowadays the politicization of privatizations does not generally take the form of simply trying to make as much money as possible. Most often it is concerned with providing favours for particular supporters of the regime, such as security officials in Mozambique, senior military men in Madagascar and Nigeria, or various local elites, such as in Nigeria, where 75 per cent of privatizations, until 1988–9, took place simply by transferring the ownership of public enterprises from the federal government to regional governments, and also in Cameroon. Sometimes political motives are more deeply hidden. In Côte d'Ivoire, the dazzling rise of François Bakou, director of the Octide group, highly regarded by the World Bank because of his strong opposition to public monopolies, cannot be explained without reference to the powerful political and even financial support he receives from the head of state, anxious to destabilize his former rival Alassane Ouattara.

In political struggles of this sort, privatizations can be an ideal weapon in an ethnic power game, even if the prime purpose remains political. In Tanzania and Uganda, rivalries of this sort have pitted Indian and Pakistani minorities against local elites. In Zimbabwe, the government has made a public demonstration of backing black citizens. In Cameroon, privatization measures have been used quite blatantly to prevent the emergence of elites likely to oppose the current government. This was the case with the privatization of the Banque internationale pour l'Afrique occidentale (BIAO) in 1991, of Minoterie in Douala and of Pamol, in all of which cases the government's principal aim was to keep these assets out of the hands of Bamileke entrepreneurs. In the case of the cotton-growing company SODECOTON, the privatization was manipulated by the government in such a way as to cause political embarrassment to a specific group of politicians of northern origin. In Nigeria, privatization measures have been enacted in such a manner as to exclude prominent southern business people, regarded as potential financiers of political parties opposed to the military government.

If privatizations are the subject of such intense manoeuvres, it is hardly on account of the attraction which the privatized assets represent in themselves. As was the case with a previous generation of nationalizations and with the management of public or parastatal enterprises, it is not the normal commercial activity of the company which constitutes the real interest in a transaction of this sort, but the possibilities which it offers to perform all manner of irregular operations and to extend one's field of influence in general. Sometimes, privatized companies produce no more than the minimum return required to finance other activities which are far more lucrative, in particular that of importing goods, an activity of the greatest social and political importance in Africa.

The economy of plunder lends itself easily to the development of criminal activities. There is only a small step necessary to the practice of using privatized companies for purposes of money-laundering or providing a cover for other sorts of illicit activity, such as with certain hotels in Senegal. A measure of privatization may serve as an occasion for simple theft, such as through the appropriation of land in Mozambique and Cameroon.

Liberalization of the banking system and the growth of financial fraud: The weakness of the banking system also contributes to the process of criminalization. Its problems are the direct consequence of the existence of the economy of plunder which we have briefly described. There is a high level of dubious bank loans made to public and parastatal companies and, in some countries, of loans made to the purchasers of privatized companies which are destined never to be repaid. The weakness of the banking system is also a result of another feature of economies of plunder, namely, the use of banks, particularly those in which the state has a majority shareholding, as sources of revenue in themselves. According to the World Bank (1995: 55), 'In the 1980s, there was widespread financial distress. Loan loss ratios were 40–60 percent, with some banks recording non-performing loans for more than 90 percent of their portfolio. Benin and Guinea experienced a complete collapse of their banking sectors in 1985–89; and several other countries faced severe instability and the collapse of individual institutions.'

This situation is not exceptional, either historically or geographically. Many countries such as Congo-Brazzaville, Chad and the Central African Republic have banking systems which are today in the last throes of collapse. The main reasons for this are the use of banking institutions for political purposes and the volume of 'high-risk loans', a euphemism for risks which are not only high but of various sorts. The high-risk category includes loans which become uncollectable due to the theft of relevant documents or arson; large sums withdrawn over the counter by senior bank officials; loans made to leading politicians which will never be repaid; loans made under cover of forged documents; the creation of companies purely as a means of gaining access to loans and which rapidly go bankrupt; the forging of details of accounts and of the operating capital of banks; the diversion of funds intended to improve a bank's liquidity, and so on.

Liberalization has not brought any fundamental improvement in this general state of affairs other than to change the precise mechanisms and locations where fraud occurs. On the contrary, the weakening of regulatory mechanisms and the disappearance of the need to provide any economic justification for money transfers, the introduction of a general freedom to change and transfer currencies and capital (Article 8 of the IMF), the possibilities created for specialist banks to operate in new markets, the mushrooming of small bureaux de change, the liberalization of both internal and foreign trade, and sometimes the modification of the political context, such as with the return of refugees to Guinea and the end of official discrimination against foreign minorities in Tanzania, have all created new opportunities for company fraud. One sign of this is the spectacular growth in fictitious assets since the mid-1980s. Financial liberalization has also blurred the frontiers between what is and is not legal by facilitating the transfer of capital and property from the illegal to the legal sector and vice versa. In particular it has made it much easier to circulate capital of illegal origin (stemming from the drug trade, corruption and over-invoicing) in the legal economy by reducing controls on the origin of funds and by diminishing the need to prove the necessity of capital transfers. In Senegal, statements made by Ahmed Califa Niasse,[1] an important leader of the Tijaniyya brotherhood as well as a leading businessman close to the most powerful circles, including by marriage into the Senghor family, are symptomatic of a practice which is now common in several countries: the granting of 'non-reimbursable loans in return for services rendered during political campaigns' is an important instrument of clientelism in Africa.

The role which central banks have played in these developments is crucial. This takes a different form depending on whether the central bank is a member of the franc zone or not. In the franc zone, central banks play more of a passive than an active role, if only because of the existence of a significant number of commercial banks. The passivity of the banking commissions of the Banque des Etats d'Afrique centrale (BEAC) and of the Banque centrale des Etats d'Afrique de l'Ouest (BCEAO) results in a high degree of tolerance in certain circumstances where negligence and even criminal behaviour might be suspected, such as their failure to react in the face of the criminal activities of banks such as the BCCI or Meridien and of the practice of charging commissions for certain money transfers. The fact is that the governors of the CFA central banks and, even more strikingly, of their various national offices are often leading political actors, who may turn a blind eye to loans of doubtful creditworthiness made by commercial banks. Outside the franc zone, commissions of inquiry into bank collapses or banking scandals have demonstrated that some central bank officials have received commissions for the management of money transfers or the purchase of foreign currency. In the same way, the awarding of banking licences can be an occasion for major corruption.

There are two main areas in which this state of affairs has direct consequences. First, banks become unwilling to grant new loans

---

[1] 'La confession de l'ayatollah de Kaolack: "La démocratie est en faillite, il n'y a plus d'argent pour nous acheter" ', *Le Figaro*, 27 December 1994.

because old loans are still costing them money. Provisions for losses are high, and interest rates on loans and overdrafts are higher than necessary as a result. Banks are unable to take legal action to recover outstanding loans in cases where a general climate of impunity reigns and where the judicial system can be corrupted. Secondly, as a result of the bankruptcy of the banking system and the unwillingness or inability of either foreign owners or the relevant monetary authorities to recapitalize local banks, and after the general withdrawal of major international banks such as the Banque Nationale de Paris, the Société Générale or Crédit Lyonnais from some countries of the franc zone, it tends to be only the most dubious and least scrupulous commercial banks which remain in Africa. These are increasingly tolerated for lack of anything better.

In recent years, the banking system has followed a disturbing course which has pushed part of the sector further into the criminal economy. Aid donors have been slow to draw the appropriate conclusions from this development, and in particular to note the role played by banks whose viability is open to doubt. In this regard, the collapse of BCCI revealed a pattern of fraud by private enterprises (since the BCCI had the almost explicit goal of facilitating any sort of illicit operation, particularly in Africa, when it had the blessing of those in power). Hence, the BCCI débâcle gave a rare insight into all manner of illegal operations carried out in various African countries, providing us with a list of some of the main procedures of economic and financial criminalization.

The main method used by BCCI was simply the purchase of influence, not only in economic and financial sectors but also in regard to religion, charitable activity, the labour market and education, sexual services, and other fields. This technique is not unique to BCCI. All banks operating in Africa have to indulge in the purchase of influence to some degree or other. All over the continent, influence is a commodity like any other, and it may be traded like any other.

More concretely, inquiries into the collapse of BCCI have revealed at least eight types of operation which developed in the banking sector in the 1980s.[2] These are listed below. All these eight types have in common the fact that they tend to benefit senior officials and politicians to the detriment, in most cases, of the state which they are appointed to serve (examples 1–6). However, certain techniques may act to the detriment of local economic actors (example 7) or foreign ones (example 8).

1. *The arrangement of a fictitious loan by BCCI to the government, or to a public or parastatal company, which requires payment of*

---

[2] The following details are taken from US Senate, *The BCCI Affair: a Report to the Committee on Foreign Relations* (US Government Printing Office, 1993), referred to here as the Kerry Report.

interest. Such an operation, which requires the state to pay interest charges, acts to the profit of BCCI and the corrupt officials who arrange it. Such cases occurred in Cameroon, where they benefited BCCI and the minister of finance of the day (Kerry Report, p. 93).

2. *The irregular administration of monies derived from the export of raw materials.* This occurred in Cameroon, where it profited some officials of the Société nationale des hydrocarbures, which generally received only some $3,000–4,000 per year, but more especially it rewarded BCCI employees who were under-reporting oil shipments and manipulating exchange rates in their own interest (Kerry Report, p. 94). In Zambia, copper exports brought handsome gains to the BCCI and local politicians when hard-currency profits were converted into local currency (Kerry Report, p. 119).

3. *Illicit financial transactions using government funds.* In many countries with inconvertible currencies, such as Nigeria and Zambia, powerful individuals were able to change government currency reserves on the black market in order to finance their election campaigns, using BCCI as an intermediary (Kerry Report, pp. 99–104, 119). The politicians agreed to the transfer of foreign-currency reserves abroad and kept the local-currency equivalent in the country. Government accounts have also been used as personal treasuries by holders of public office for speculating in currency markets and financing high-risk transactions of various kinds. In Nigeria, government funds were used for currency swaps in such a way that, if there was a loss, this was charged to the account of the state, but, if there was a profit, Nigerian officials received the first 8 percentage points and BCCI officials the rest.

4. *Under- or over-invoicing of imports and exports.* This is a practice which operates to the detriment of public bodies which pay above the market price, which receive less than the market price, or which receive smaller receipts than are justified by the real quantities of goods sold on the market, and to the benefit of BCCI and those senior officials and politicians who share the windfall gains, generally placing the profits in accounts abroad. This practice has been recorded in every African country but is especially important in Nigeria, in particular with regard to oil sold by the Nigerian National Petroleum Corporation in the United States until 1991 (Kerry Report, p. 101).

5. *The deposit in overseas accounts of the profits of fraud.* This can include monies obtained from tax evasion or tax fraud, or from other fraud whether linked to BCCI or not, and from illicit activity generally. This means of capital flight is used everywhere.

6. *The laundering of dirty money through a joint venture between a government and BCCI.* In Cameroon, a joint venture between BCCI and the government operated in favour notably of Kanga Zamb Jean, former Secretary of State at the Ministry of Finance (Kerry Report, p. 93). This was one of the circuits for laundering drug money from Latin America, made public during a major court case in Tampa, Florida.

7. *Illegal practices intended to facilitate legal operations.* This includes the bribing of central-bank employees and politicians who are influential in business circles, such as those responsible for the central bank and the ministries of the economy, finance, trade and industry, to ensure rapid handling of financial transactions and favourable official treatment generally. In Congo-Brazzaville, BCCI was one of only two banks out of 32 which were reimbursed after the restructuring of the government's debt portfolio in 1987 (Kerry Report, p. 96). In Senegal, BCCI had preferential access to foreign exchange, which enabled it to propose better terms than any of its competitors for import transactions (Kerry Report, p. 118). In Nigeria, BCCI was able, thanks to its political influence, to obtain foreign exchange two or three times more rapidly than its competitors. By the end of the 1980s it had obtained a virtual monopoly in import–export financing (Kerry Report, p. 101).

8. *The falsification of government accounts,* generally in order to facilitate economic and financial relations between a government and the international community. This type of operation occurred, using very similar procedures, in Senegal, Zambia and Nigeria. It involved an artificial inflation of the state's currency reserves or the nominal level of fiscal receipts in order to appear to conform to IMF or World Bank lending conditions, thus enabling the country to qualify for new loans or financial facilities.

Such practices do not occur only on the margins of public life. On the contrary, the illicit transactions which brought such benefit to BCCI gradually put the bank in a dominant position, to the point that it was the leading foreign bank in Africa by the time of its eventual demise. Moreover, the sums involved in such operations were sometimes enormous. Cameroon, for example, lost $90 million in 1990–1, or 25.5 billion CFA, which at that time was some 10 per cent of the total revenue of the state other than from oil sales.

Just a few years later, the saga of the Meridien group, which has today been liquidated, bears a close resemblance to that of BCCI. Both began with a period of rapid development and growth, attracting a significant level of state deposits, which in Meridien's case amounted to a quarter of its total deposits. Other practices common to both banks included the management of government funds in such a way as to benefit senior officers of the bank and some leading government officials and politicians, to the detriment of the state itself; the cultivation of close and highly ambiguous relations with the head of state in countries where they were operating; and a privileged relationship with national or regional public bodies (Meridien was the leading recipient of low-cost loans to the private sector by the African Development Bank and received from the government of Zambia, for its restructuring, $41 million in 1994). Meridien gave loans to, or acquired shares in, public companies well known to be in difficulties, had local branches of dubious reputation and offered to perform illegal transactions such as the conversion of CFA francs between the Central and West African CFA zones, while at the same time maintaining a symbiotic relationship with the ITM group of companies.

Practices of this sort are not the sole preserve of criminal organizations such as BCCI or Meridien. In 1994, Indosuez Aval Bank and American Express Bank carried out similar procedures in falsifying the accounts of the Kenyan government in order to deceive the World Bank and the IMF. Following a mission by these institutions, the government of Kenya asked the two banks, in return for payment and certain other considerations, to deposit funds with the central bank on behalf of the government so as to acquire the level of reserves necessary for the disbursement of new international funding. Under- and over-invoicing of imports are common procedures in all African states and a great number of companies participate in such practices, as do banks, often involuntarily or unconsciously because of the frequent absence of any serious audit of company accounts.

A long tradition of customs fraud and smuggling

Since the 1980s, there has been an abundance of studies of cross-border smuggling. Anthropological, political and socio-economic studies of trade networks have shown that customs fraud and smuggling form a part of foreign trade policy, just as much as protectionism does. All the historical studies of trade policy, and of the manner in which it is implemented in practice, demonstrate the importance of networks of traders, not in the sense of forming immutable institutions which resist state policy, but as leading actors in the formation of national economic policies. Some of the oldest commercial networks have played a comparable role since as long ago as the twelfth century. History also demonstrates that the straddling of positions of power and accumulation by individuals has a marked effect on the actual results of public policy interventions. Thus, while the reorganization of trade in colonial times generally served to undermine those long-distance trades which were previously in African hands, certain individual

merchants were able to benefit from the colonial trading system by acting as agents for the big European trading houses and as intermediaries of every sort, participating in the colonial economy and thus per-
petuating their old mode of existence under a new guise. This may
serve as a reminder of the deep ambivalence of various activities
which are technically classified as fraudulent.

The recent liberalization of import rules was intended to improve
the competitiveness of African economies but also to squeeze parallel
markets and to reduce the number of obstacles to international trade.
However, it now appears that liberalization has actually had the opposite effect, namely that of reinforcing informal networks. Two factors
may help to explain this.[3]

In the first place, contrary to what is supposed by supporters of
trade liberalization, it is difficult to draw clear distinctions between
formal and informal activities. Formal-sector businesses may manipulate various tariffs and may practise under-invoicing. The Alhazai of
Maradi in Niger and the religious brotherhoods in Senegal alternate
constantly between the formal and informal sectors in order to derive
the maximum profit from their activities, and the leading traders constantly switch between official and technically clandestine markets in
a form of arbitrage. The symbiosis between formal and informal operates by means of the personal and commercial networks which form
around membership of a savings club or among people from the same
village, and through kinship lines or membership of associations or
secret societies such as the Freemasons and Rosicrucians. On a macro-
economic level, entrepôt states are good illustrations of the great
ambivalence of economic behaviour and of the difficulties in ascer-
taining whether economic activity actually occurs in the legal or formal sectors. For more than a decade, a number of countries, including
Benin, Gambia, Togo, Equatorial Guinea, Burundi, Sudan and, less
systematically, Niger and Guinea, have endowed themselves with a
comparative advantage at regional level by importing goods officially
with very low tariffs and then re-exporting them, often illegally from
the point of view of the recipient country. The division into formal and
informal spheres is thus not a useful distinction in Africa, since illegal
practices are also performed in the formal sector, while so-called informal economic networks operate with well-established hierarchies and
are fully integrated into social life.

Partly as a consequence, the informal economy is closely connected
to politics. Every study based on fieldwork shows that, if many commercial networks have in fact prospered since independence, it is
partly because of the traders' relationship with states which have the

[3] For further details, see Hibou, 1996.

tangled, complex social roots so characteristic of postcolonial Africa. Relations between trade and politics can be extremely varied, going from the simple payment of tribute to total control. The alliances, implicit understandings, and other relationships between the two categories of politics and economics vary from complete identity of interests to a 'subtle balance between tolerance and repression, during the course of which the respective interests of major traders, the political and administrative institutions and the various officials who staff them are cultivated for mutual benefit' (Grégoire and Labazée, 1993: 33).

Customs evasion or smuggling, then, cannot be considered in isolation as an activity which is simply illegal or criminal, but is better seen as one among a larger variety of techniques designed to exploit opportunities offered by the state and to gain access to the profits generated by operating between the local and international sectors. In this regard, money-laundering is a practice particularly widespread in Africa. Because of the importance of the informal sector and its ties to the formal sector, the laundering of money takes place constantly, as profits drawn from the former are constantly reinvested in the latter. It is a practice as routine, as necessary and as widespread as informal activity itself. As a consequence, there is little obstacle to the recycling of profits gained in illicit business. By the same token, barter, which is commonplace in international fraud, lends itself to money-laundering through the acquisition of exportable goods, such as diamonds, gold, and antiques.

In fact, however, the comparative advantage of sub-Saharan Africa in money-laundering is quite limited by comparison with the traditional off-shore banking centres of the Caribbean and Western Europe, and even with some of the world's major economies. Africa, subject as it is to economic and political crisis, does not offer many attractions by comparison. Thus, several of the scandals which in recent years have shaken the African financial world, such as the collapse of BCCI and Meridien, and the cases of 'parallel financing' in the Central African Republic, Congo and Madagascar, are perhaps better considered as fraud on the grand scale or as blatant attempts at siphoning national resources than as money-laundering operations.

Nevertheless, sub-Saharan economies present at least one peculiarity which is worthy of further attention: namely, they are the last in the world to function almost entirely with cash, and they represent a particularly favourable point of entry into the international banking system, all the more so in that fiscal and customs agencies, central and commercial banks, accounting firms, and the laws and regulations in force are all generally porous in the extreme. Different markets or sectors of the economy are well suited to the conversion of cash of dubious origin into legal goods or properties. It is virtually public knowledge that real estate in Senegal and Nigeria, hotels in Senegal, Côte d'Ivoire, Equatorial Guinea and Kenya, casinos in South Africa, Namibia, Gabon, Cameroon, Côte d'Ivoire and, perhaps shortly, Senegal, betting on French horse races through the Pari mutuel urbain (PMU) system, and the national lottery in various countries of the franc zone, works of art in Cameroon, Angola and former Zaïre, fisheries in Guinea, the vanilla trade in Madagascar, bureaux de change in Nigeria and commercial banks in Nigeria, Liberia and Benin, an import–export trade which makes systematic use of product dumping (Nigeria) and the import of luxury cars (Nigeria again) all fulfil such a function. The oil spot market, formidably complex and supplied by a multitude of front companies, appears well suited to the recycling of dubious capital whenever production statistics are kept virtually secret as much by international oil companies as by national ones, as in Nigeria, even though some oil industry experts believe that the spot market does not play precisely this role. The diamond market is closely controlled by De Beers and the intimate network of Antwerp diamond dealers, and it concerns a product whose value is too artificial and its margins too narrow for it to act as a massive money laundry in the way that some commentators have suggested,[4] although the diamond trade does permit predatory operations and fraud on a huge scale on the part of the main traders, often Israeli and Lebanese, and by holders of political or military power, such as in former Zaïre, Angola, Liberia, Sierra Leone and the Central African Republic. Forged import documents are increasingly used to recycle dirty money directly via the banking system, for example in Côte d'Ivoire, where fictitious imports and re-exports of cloth to the rest of the region take place in quantities quite out of proportion to the size of the market. One Ivorian supplier, for example, declared himself to have imported such an enormous quantity of shoes that, in order to sell them, he would have had to sell five or six pairs a year per head of the population. The same principle may lead to the formal establishment of paper businesses which are actually non-existent, such as pharmacies in Cameroon.

The trend towards economic liberalization which began in the early 1980s is occurring in a context of institutional decay which favours all manner of money-laundering, less through financial markets, where the rules are too restrictive, than by direct investment, for example in the privatization of state companies and especially in the more or less fictitious accounting practised in newly privatized businesses, or under cover of export-processing zones and free ports. In practice, the origin of capital invested in this way and the reality of reported capital or commercial flows go unchecked. Few places in Africa have satisfactory

---

[4] A scandal in the Antwerp diamond market in 1997 has provided evidence which might suggest that this opinion is in need of some qualification.

procedures for auditing company accounts. Loss-making companies are particularly useful since they can serve as covers for regular transfers of money without any form of control. This is one field in which Africa is remarkably competitive.

In general, there are good reasons to suppose that, for those who have funds of dubious origin which they wish to launder, sub-Saharan Africa is simply a point of entry into the international system. Capital introduced in this way does not really contribute to the development of productive capacity, contrary to the case in Colombia and some Asian countries. Hence, Africa's role in the laundering of drug money should not be exaggerated. In his testimony to a hearing of the US Senate sub-committee on African affairs, Robert S. Gelbard, the Assistant Secretary of State for international narcotics and law enforcement affairs, estimated on 20 July 1995 that Nigeria was 'not a major money-laundering center'. It appears most likely, then, that African drug traders do not repatriate profits they have earned in America and Europe. Moreover, it would indeed be odd if they, of all people, were to go against the general rule in Africa, which is to move capital out of the continent. The most that can be said is that some cases of commercial dumping via exports or re-exports from Nigeria to the franc zone, and the import of luxury cars and electronic goods to Nigeria, may be suspected of forming part of a money-laundering cycle. However, the use of Africa as a point of transit for drug profits en route to Western banking centres could well increase in the years to come if the IMF succeeds in persuading the countries of the CFA franc zone to renounce their adherence to Article 14 of the IMF, which contains a derogation from the principle of the total liberty of currency transfers, and to apply instead Article 8, and if the World Bank succeeds in liberalizing the business environment still further. International operators with dubious credentials have established bases south of the Sahara and their positions there could grow rapidly in importance in favourable circumstances. This would include the Corsican underworld which is established in Cameroon, Gabon, Congo and Côte d'Ivoire, Italian crime syndicates in Kenya, Somalia, Seychelles and Senegal; Russians and Ukrainians in Guinea, Sierra Leone and South Africa; and Asians in East Africa.

Fraudulent practices are all the more common in that they are an economic necessity. Ivory and gold, regarded for centuries as sources of revenue and suitable forms for saving or raising capital or for use in the acquisition of other goods, in other words as forms of money, are today, for certain groups of people, virtually the only link between the local and international economies in situations where currencies are unconvertible, and where hard currency is scarce or is allocated only to those with political connections. This appears to have been one of the most significant features of the gold and ivory traffic which Burundi at one stage had succeeded in capturing from all of East Africa.

There is often a link between smuggling and other forms of illicit activity. Thus, during the 1970s, the drug trade developed in Italy in the hands of smuggling gangs run by the Camorra which had previously specialized in trafficking in cigarettes. This development took place notably on account of the fact that both activities made use of the same financial channels. In Colombia, drug networks first developed from among structures earlier established in the emerald smuggling trade. We have already noted that drug trafficking in Nigeria is mainly in the hands of Ibo groups, which are well connected to networks engaged in general-purpose smuggling, the illicit manufacture of patented goods, counterfeit currency trading and credit-card fraud. In Mozambique, one important businessman from the Indian sub-continent, with excellent connections to leading politicians, was recently implicated in a case of smuggling hashish hidden in cargoes of other goods, principally tea. But drug trafficking is not the only such trade which is worthy of note. According to the US government, the theft of food aid is now one of the major means of self-enrichment in Africa. Theft of this nature is well organized in various countries by officials or armed organizations, and it has a clear place in the whole gamut of illegal cross-frontier activities. In the Zambezi valley, for example, it is organized by the same people who control the smuggling of ivory and rhinoceros horn: 25 per cent of aid landed in Mozambique for drought relief in Zambia and Zimbabwe is said to have been diverted. In the same way, the trade in stolen vehicles, whose routes originally developed from those used for the smuggling of second-hand cars, is said by Interpol to be among Africa's most important branches of criminal commerce, second only to drugs.

The effects of economic and financial extraversion

The export of primary products and la politique du ventre: Since they specialize in the export of a small range of primary products, African countries are particularly susceptible to a management of their main economic resources which is highly politicized and centrally controlled. This is particularly the case with regard to mining and oil production. The extraction of minerals in enclave centres of production, sometimes off-shore, enables the political authorities to negotiate royalties and other agreements directly with major companies. According to oil industry experts, OPEC countries on average retain some 75 per cent of their oil revenues for the state budget, allowing for operating expenses. But, in the case of African oil producers, this proportion is closer, even in the best cases, to the range of 55–70 per cent. The difference represents a supplementary profit shared by the oil companies and African elites. In the current period of pressure on middlemen's profit margins, the oil companies appear to have a working agreement that they should try to reduce the size of commissions offered for the allocation of contracts, while at the same time themselves maintaining profit margins higher than they are able to obtain in other continents. In much the same way, De Beers is reported to have signed production and marketing contracts in Africa which are more favourable to the company than is possible in other parts of the world.

Similar practices may be identified in the management of the uranium mines of Niger, phosphates in Togo, and bauxite and aluminium in Guinea. Only a meagre revenue reaches the state treasury, or even none at all, while the real royalties are paid directly to politicians in foreign bank accounts.

When the physical characteristics of a business do not easily permit such a tight political management of the production and marketing process, the state may create an infrastructure which enables it to maintain some degree of central control. In the marketing of agricultural products on which a tax may be charged, such as groundnuts, cocoa and coffee, the creation of marketing boards or other regulatory mechanisms in every African country was for a long period a reflection of this preoccupation with central control. Some countries have become highly specialized in the concentration in one central point of export resources from a wide area. Burundi, for example, drew significant state revenue from government-licensed ivory-dealing offices in the 1970s and 1980s, and from gold-trading bureaux in the 1990s, although it produces negligible quantities of both commodities. Of the gold which it exported in the 1990s, 80 per cent actually originated in Zaïre and 19 per cent in Tanzania and Uganda.

In cases such as these, the strategy of the most powerful politicians is once more best viewed in a historical light. African potentates have always striven to acquire or maintain a monopoly of foreign relations and have often been prepared to accept relatively unfavourable economic and financial conditions in order to keep an exclusive control of this sector and prevent their domestic rivals from developing relations with abroad. This was true, for example, at the time of the trans-Atlantic commerce of the eighteenth and nineteenth centuries. The constant tendency of the price of slaves to fall was less a function of supply and demand than a reflection of the growing dependence of African elites on imported trade goods and of the growth in internal political conflicts associated with the trade and its management (Miller, 1988). The current situation recalls rather more accurately the economy of the colonial entrepôts, known as factories, which was characteristic of the late nineteenth century. The modern trades in diamonds, hardwood, rubber and various minerals display a similar pattern, being organized in a series of enclaves. Still more striking is the comparison between earlier and contemporary arrangements on the part of foreign businessmen and African elites at the expense of the population of Africa in general. Some countries demonstrate a remarkable similarity with older patterns in the way in which violence is organized and private police forces deployed.

Trade liberalization has actually made little impact in this area. The dismantling of the main regulatory agencies and marketing boards and the privatization of various mining enterprises have done little to disturb the organization of the main economic resources of the continent, which were already effectively privatized. The same economic operators, very often foreign, and the same political actors continue to control these sectors.

A form of organization which is centralized, is subject to close political control and is de facto in private hands lends itself particularly well to the criminalization of African economies. Financial arrangements between foreign entrepreneurs and African strong men often have important political implications. In Burundi for example, the struggle for control of the most important purchasing offices has been a factor in the development of the civil war. At the height of this rivalry, in 1994, one minister was assassinated on account of certain controversial positions he had taken. The three main gold-purchasing bureaux in Burundi are all connected to specific politicians and have financed political factions or parties, especially extremist ones, and have thus made a direct contribution to the funding of massacres. In former Zaïre, where the diamond business is organized in a similar way in a small number of purchasing offices, diamonds have served in the laundering of counterfeit zaïre banknotes printed without the imprimatur of the Ministry of Finance. Sometimes they have been used for laundering counterfeit dollars. In spite of the technical complexity and the highly organized nature of oil markets, it may be suspected that officials of the Nigerian National Petroleum Corporation (NNPC) have laundered drug money, thanks to the opacity of the NNPC's management and the impossibility of acquiring data on the volume of goods it exports.

A non-viable fiscal system: The principle of extraversion also operates in fiscal matters. African countries are characterized by the weakness of their internal tax-gathering systems and by the importance of taxes levied on their external relations, such as imports, exports and remittances by foreign companies.

The importance of taxes on foreign trade has a long tradition in African economies. Nowadays, it poses a serious problem since foreign trade liberalization policies are leading to a decline in this source of revenue which is so essential for the state budget. At the same time, this particular source of state revenue, the only one easily accessible to weakened administrations, has for decades been eroded through the growth of customs fraud and smuggling. All this is taking place at a time when the growing burden of debt requires states to raise more revenue.

The fact that the weakness of internal revenue collection is due in the first instance to the extraversion of the economy should not lead us to underestimate the internal reasons why African states have such difficulties in raising income. These domestic factors include the high number of people who are exempted from paying taxes for political reasons, which is the consequence of a high degree of fiscal indiscipline stemming from the lack of legitimacy of public authorities. Recent reforms of internal revenue systems have not had very impressive results because they are unable to tackle problems which are strongly political and social in nature. Attempts to impose value-added tax have failed because of the size and the ingenuity of the informal economy. Attempts to create more consistent tax regimes clash with the socio-political logic which leads to tax exemptions and other forms of favouritism. Measures to maximize tax revenue by putting collection in the hands of foreign companies have led to a further exaggeration of the dual nature of the fiscal system and thus aggravate one of the underlying causes of weak internal fiscal control. In Côte d'Ivoire, for example, the current reform policy, which aims to create a single agency with responsibility for collecting taxes from major companies, is explicitly based on a strategy of levying internal taxes on the formal part of the economy and thus, ostensibly at least, of leaving untaxed the greater part of the country's real economy. This reorganization, motivated as it is by a wish for short-term efficiency, may in the longer run perpetuate the under-fiscalization of both African entrepreneurs and African consumers.

Once more the weight of history is considerable. Before the colonial period, in the absence of states with highly centralized institutions, the raising and payment of tax were seen as a form of tribute and submission. Those who refused to submit to the payment of taxes and tributes to a dominant power were liable to become the targets of armed raids. During the colonial period, tax collection was more or less privatized. Traditional chiefs often abused their position to divert the taxes which they collected or to demand extra taxes without the knowledge of their colonial masters. In those days the major part of central government tax revenues actually came from colonial companies and from customs receipts. Today, as in the past, payment of taxes is not considered an expression of the state's domestic sovereignty and legitimacy, but is perceived by the general public as the expression of the state's international sovereignty (in the form of taxes on foreigners and trans-border trade flows) and as a manifestation of its coercive power. This is demonstrated by the principle of taxing the weak, the recalcitrant and whoever is not connected directly to those in power.

The lack of a culture of tax-paying and the high incidence of embezzlement have acquired their current proportions only because those primarily responsible have enjoyed an effective impunity for decades. It is for this reason that the current fiscal system constitutes both an illustration and a component of that part of Africa's social capital which has a high propensity to criminalization. It is flagrant in Côte d'Ivoire, for example, which is nevertheless often cited as a model of correct behaviour. Senior officials, often cited as tax evaders, show no embarrassment in publicly celebrating the fact of becoming CFA franc billionaires.

The importance of revenue drawn from foreign sources reflects the central place of rents derived from external relations and the economic and political role of mediation in African systems of political economy. These characteristics are a reflection of the specific forms which the state has taken in Africa over a long period and the vagaries of the legitimacy and authority enjoyed by its current governments.

The privatization of the administration

The factor which has most contributed to the development of activities internationally considered as improper or illegal, and to the abuse of reforms for various semi-legal or illegal purposes, is the erosion of public administration. This has in fact been hastened by various foreign interventions in a thoroughly ambiguous manner.

The state and its alter ego
Contrary to what World Bank and IMF documents would have us believe, not to mention the press and a good part of the academic literature, African countries are not characterized by the weakness of the state, its foreign origin or its inability to organize societies. However, while the state is securely rooted in the realities of African life, it certainly does take some very particular forms. These are described by Jean-François Bayart (1993) as a 'rhizome state' and William Reno (1995) as a 'shadow state'.

The origins of the rhizome state – so called because of its metaphorical resemblance to a tangled underground root system – lie in its colonial predecessor. The insecurity of the colonizers and the relative weakness of their resources have shaped African states in such a way that the relationships, institutions and people most prominently in public view are not necessarily the most powerful. Elements which at first sight appear to be obstacles to the functioning of the state may turn out, on closer inspection, actually to belong to the state. Such is the case with Touba, the holy city of the Mourides, better known as a centre for contraband and as the most economically dynamic city in Senegal. But Touba is not at all a centre of opposition to the state. It actually forms part of the informal state structure (or more accurately, of the ensemble formed by the formal state and its informal shadow) via a web of informal concessions, carefully negotiated privileges – notably including impunity for economic offences – and personal and political relationships.

All over Africa, the state participates actively in the informal economy, especially in matters affecting international trade. This has already been discussed above with reference to imports. Naturally enough, the same applies to exports. In Uganda, *magendo*, that is, the illegal export of products, is not organized by people who stand outside the governing circle. The links between officially unrecognized or illegal markets and those controlled by the state are so clear that it is reasonable to consider *magendo* to be an instrument in the formation of a new dominant social class. In Zimbabwe, the traffic in ivory and rhinoceros horn has involved not only guerrilla movements but also the military authorities. In general, illegal diamond exports are not carried out by small-time diggers or traders but by those at the highest reaches of power.

Nor is the implication of the state in the 'informal' or 'illegal' sectors limited to the import–export business. It is characteristic of every sphere in which the state intervenes in Africa, as much in economic relations of exchange and production as in political and social relations. In Cameroon and Gabon, poaching has become very widespread in recent years, thanks to the complicity of leading personalities, military men and senior officials. In every African country it is at the level of the elites that the lack of a culture of tax-paying is most highly developed. One report by the French Ministry of Co-operation regarding property taxes in Côte d'Ivoire, for example, underlined the fact that Cocody, the wealthiest area of Abidjan, is also the suburb with the lowest proportion of income tax collection, with a 3 per cent recovery ratio. Reports made by companies specialized in the recovery of bad loans on behalf of banks in the process of liquidation or restructuring show that such loans are mainly to members of the national elite, who invariably neglect to repay them.

We should not conclude from this that harmony and concord reign in an informal sector which has now become generalized, for the intrusion of the state in the informal sector does nothing to prevent conflict. To take the example of Senegal once more, the rise in tension between Touba and Dakar does not arise from the emancipation of a reinvigorated civil society faced with an enfeebled state. Rather, it simply reveals the absence of homogeneity in a rhizome-like state. As in any organization, bouts of dissidence, tension and negotiation are a fact of life. This fragmentation of power is the source of constant new conflicts such as bitter inter-faction disputes over privatization, and is marked by periodic official campaigns against smuggling and corruption, which always target very specific groups. Episodes such as these reveal to public gaze the balance of forces and the alliances of the moment. When opportunities or situations arise for making money these can frequently result in crises, open conflicts, the break-up of coalitions and the renegotiation of alliances. Such a battle of rival factions is currently taking place in Cameroon around the issue of privatizing INTELCAM, pitting the Secretary-General of the Presidency against the Minister of Posts and Telecommunications. Another battle royal in Cameroon concerns the contribution to be made by public-sector companies to the financing of the summit of the Organization of African Unity held in Yaoundé in May 1996 and their contribution to the state budget. In this contest the Minister of the Economy was confronted by the Secretary-General of the Presidency, who sought to wrest control of these contributions, reportedly so as to facilitate an over-invoicing scheme connected with the purchase of computers. In the extreme case of Sierra Leone, William Reno has shown how the recent war has its roots in the aggravation of such centrifugal forces existing at the heart of the state. In this particular case, opposition and conflict between rival networks took increasingly violent forms over a period of years, leading to war. State interventions can certainly be more subtle than this. Examples would include the tolerance of the public authorities in the face of every form of illegality, the state's turning a blind eye to illegal sources of revenue, and the indulgence with which justice is sometimes administered.

By this point of the discussion, we hope to have demonstrated that the specific nature of the state in Africa goes far to explain why the results of economic reforms do not conform to the results predicted by the economic models used in their design, with specific reference to measures of privatization and financial and trade liberalization, to the dismantling of marketing boards and the reform of the tax structure. It may be noted that some authors have made similar findings regarding other continents. Measures of liberalization and deregulation produce few of the effects predicted and many unexpected ones in cases where economic relations are dominated not by markets but by specific networks of operators, in which case economic regulation is effected less by the law and by formal rules than by personal prestige and the strength of private relationships. The impact and significance of such unexpected consequences of reform are all the more telling when there exist informal institutions which have the ability to slow the process of reforms and even to transform them into something radically different from what was intended by their designers.

For similar reasons, the specific nature of states is also a cause of the lack of success of the institutional and administrative reforms suggested or imposed by the aid donor community.

The erosion of administration

Although we have argued that the state in Africa has deep roots, it none the less remains true that public administration and institutions in Africa are indeed weak, as a result of the rhizome-like nature of the state and of the organization of public power in general. Administrative procedures and legislative or institutional rules are only one channel among many which the public authorities use to manage the country's affairs. Personal relations and personal networks, whether of an economic, political, religious or regional nature, frequently offer far more effective instruments of public management.

The aid donor community is unquestionably correct in pointing to the existence of institutional weaknesses and other administrative shortcomings. These failings have been aggravated in recent years by the combination of an economic crisis and the particularly disastrous way in which it has been managed. The great paradox is that they have been made still worse by the severity of structural adjustment policies and their particular brand of ambivalence and by the concomitant development of corruption. Such is the gravity of this effect that today it has become accurate to speak of the collapse of public administration.

Since the mid-1980s, the rapid decline in the standard of living of civil servants, the virtual disappearance of operational budgets, frequent delays in the payment of salaries, the feeling of insecurity which now pervades elites and their consequent haste to enrich themselves, and the climate of total impunity have all conspired to cause a fall in the productivity of public officials. This was already low owing to the widespread practice of civil servants taking second jobs, the loss of their various allowances, the habit of charging for the performance of official duties, corruption, the erosion of accepted standards of public administration and the decline in the prestige of the state generally. In these circumstances economic reform measures are sometimes negotiated clumsily, by African civil servants who are poorly prepared for important meetings and who lack viable statistics. In some cases they may have a distinctly ambiguous attitude to the application of reforms, such as when officials responsible for implementing reforms are not the same as those who have negotiated them, which can lead to misunderstandings and evasions. The relaxation or abolition of controls of various sorts encourages the development of corruption and a general administrative laxity, and enhances the opportunities for discretionary interventions. The latter are made easier because of the existence of various administrative loopholes, the weakness of the judicial system, and the facility with which the complexity and uncertainty inherent in any transitional situation can be exploited.

If the need for administrative and institutional reorganization is beyond question, the reforms implemented or attempted until now have failed because they are based on incorrect theoretical foundations. These can be summarized in six main postulates.

Postulate no. 1: To reduce corruption, it is necessary to reduce the opportunities for discretionary intervention by the government. The problem here is that the relation between corruption and the incidence of discretionary interventions in government is not at all simple. At first sight, and according to standard economic theory, discretionary interventions in the economy are conducive to corruption, and it is for this reason that a maximum degree of consistency and uniformity is desirable. But experience appears to suggest that corruption may also permit the introduction of discretionary interventions and flexibility when these qualities are absent (Tanzi, 1995). The attempt to suppress discretionary state interventions appears thus not only to be utopian and unlikely to succeed, but also little suited to tackling the problems of corruption and criminalization.

Postulate no. 2: In order to counter the scale of embezzlement and lack of rigour in the administration of funds, aid donors should apply greater pressure and more detailed conditionality. However, such conditionality, when applied to rhizome-like states and in the context of the erosion of government which has taken place in Africa, has often had results which are the opposite of those intended. In the 1980s, for example, pressure from the IMF and the World Bank on Sierra Leone actually pushed the government further along the road of illegality by causing it to adopt closer links with some of the less scrupulous Lebanese traders in the President's entourage. These businessmen in fact represented the only option for the government if it was to conform to the conditions to which it was required to submit. Foreign business associates alone had the ability and the funds to purchase companies earmarked for privatization. They succeeded, by a variety of means, in supplying the minimum level of receipts required by the national budget, since the international donors asked few questions about the origin of such funds, while Lebanese banks and businesses were accepting capital from illicit sources. Lebanese traders were able to find new private-sector foreign partners, some of them unscrupulous enough to invest in Sierra Leone while engaging in illegal activities.

Postulate no. 3: Faced with the resistance of African actors, the important thing is to reach consensus. This urge to compromise on the part of aid donors may be explained by bureaucratic logic, such as the wish of individual functionaries to further their careers, and by the sheer momentum acquired by large organizations. There are also political factors, including pressure from important bilateral partners such as France in the franc-zone countries and the donors' fear of provoking civil wars or disorder. But the reasons for compromise are above all financial. Suppliers of aid credits are obsessed with securing repayment. A similar preoccupation exists, in slightly different form, among non-governmental organizations concerned at all costs to achieve the highest possible financial turnover, competing with each other and constantly seeking to enhance their prestige. (In passing, we may note that this recalls one of the most prominent features of colonial government. For metropolitan bureaucracies, it was essential to impose some financial discipline on their colonial administrations and to encourage them to run a balanced budget so as to save the metropole as far as possible from having to subsidize them. Meanwhile, officials based in the colonies themselves were concerned above all with safeguarding their personal careers.) These factors explain why it is that aid donors are often willing to accept unorthodox arrangements, and sometimes shoddy or half-baked measures, and are ready to agree to almost any stop-gap. They often neglect to penalize abuses or sub-standard performances and sometimes ally themselves more or less directly with people and networks who are at the heart of illicit practices. In this way aid donors too develop relations of an informal nature with African states. Whether conscious or not, all of these attitudes have as an unintended consequence the strengthening of the tangled root-systems of African states, some of whose subterranean offshoots extend to criminal activity. By the same means, donors actually encourage the development of personal networks, of informal or even illegal practices, and, most particularly, they weaken institutions. This also gradually leads the aid donors themselves to develop relations of an unwholesome type. The World Bank and the IMF claim that certain criteria are being observed and close their eyes to the origin of various funds or the manner in which certain privatizations are carried out. In short, this strategy reinforces those networks of the state which are the most inclined towards criminality, encourages the erosion of government and stimulates a propensity to deceive and to falsify.

It is in these factors that we find the explanation for apparently paradoxical types of behaviour. We may cite as an example the fact that it is at the moment when a crisis becomes most evident that external finances flow most easily, giving an impetus to the development of illegal activities and the erosion of a government's administrative capacity. This was true of Zaïre, Sierra Leone and Liberia in the 1980s, and nowadays it is the case with Cameroon.

Postulate no. 4: To discourage the growth of the informal sector and of illegality, the tendency of the public authorities or of the government to intervene in the economy in any form should be reduced. According to standard economic analysis, over-active or inappropriate intervention by a government creates a reaction in the form of enhanced informal or even illegal economic activity and the development of parallel markets, which attempt to mimic the action of perfect markets in a situation where the state plays a minimum role. However, close observation of the way in which parallel markets work, and of the behaviour of informal-sector operators, as well as of the actual process of liberalization, shows that the informal sector is certainly not the outward expression of market forces, in opposition to the state. The interconnection of the formal and the informal is a deeply embedded feature of the way in which African economies are organized. Hence, informal and illegal economic behaviour cannot be considered solely as the consequence of insufficient liberalization, since the real reasons for these things are more complex. Business confidence in parallel economic circuits is often greater than that in formal ones, because the former are more deeply embedded in the social structure. Nowadays there can be no serious doubt that the informal mode of conducting economic transactions is more expeditious than its formal equivalent. Main sources of supply for informal trade circuits, such as South-East Asia and the free ports of the Middle East, are often better suited to the purchasing power of informal entrepreneurs than the European sources of supply to formal markets. Incentives to enter the formal market structure, such as the abolition of formal restrictions and the lowering of fiscal charges, are outweighed by incentives to stay in the informal sector. These include the belief that recent improvements in formal regulations are short-term and precarious, the fact that public administration is increasingly inefficient, the greater ease of under-invoicing, and the risk of falling foul of changes in the official rules governing formal transactions, plus the fact that many people simply have more confidence in quasi-traditional networks and greater mastery of the methods of management and finance which they entail.

Postulate no. 5: To reinforce the effectiveness of government and encourage the development of the rule of law, new measures and legal reforms are required. Every close analysis of the way in which African economies actually operate shows that official laws are ignored, whatever their quality, and that the main factor leading people to behave as they do is precisely the wish to evade these laws. It is not the inadequacy of the law which is the point at issue but the fact that people systematically flout it. Both old and new laws meet the same fate. In other words, the function of laws is to act as objective measures of what is to be evaded or avoided, the fixed points around which new procedures are constantly developing.

Postulate no. 6: While waiting for reforms to take full effect, donors should strengthen whatever core of effectiveness exists, even if it is iso-

lated, within the government. This is a strategy adopted with increasing frequency by aid donors in Africa because of the slowness of adjustment and the doggedness of resistance to it. For example, in Cameroon, an approach of this sort took the form of concentrating on negotiations with the team led by Justin Nidoro, Minister of the Economy until September 1996. (We may note that Nidoro's team was mostly composed of informal appointees.) At first sight the results were quite encouraging, since this small group was able to produce a significant number of new laws and plans of action. In reality, such a technocratic strategy simply contributes to the further erosion of government. In the first place, it demobilizes still further other parts of the government, which are greatly superior in number. Secondly, it isolates those technocrats identified by the donors as their partners from the concrete difficulties which will be encountered in applying new measures, and notably from the political conflicts which they will cause. Thirdly, this strategy hastens the loss of legitimacy of the civil service. Fourthly, it encourages the creation of shadow economic and administrative structures.

Partly as a result of strategies of this type, government no longer functions in a normal way in many countries today. In the absence of any clear rules, and faced by a multiplicity of strategies, directives and lines of authority, civil servants in a state of thorough confusion are often unable to form any clear idea of the consequences of their actions. The climate of uncertainty encourages corruption and leads to deviant forms of individual behaviour and a general erosion of standards. The deterioration in the quality of African civil services is nowadays such that it has become materially and humanly impossible to implement reforms. Any attempt to do so immediately provokes resistance and the invention of a whole range of new strategems of deception.

The effect of the attitudes and presuppositions of aid donors on this process is far from negligible. Although the donors were not, of course, the ones who set this train of events in motion, they nevertheless bear a large responsibility for aggravating and prolonging it. They reinforce the tendency of African states to develop underground roots, including through their propensity to illegality, by encouraging the informal dimension and the power of personal networks in the widest sense, by financing faction leaders and those in positions of power and by giving them external legitimation, among other things. Furthermore, donors actively participate in the further splintering of existing centres of state power, and the reforms currently in progress have in fact unwittingly contributed to diminishing the visible symbols and even the substance of public authority. One of the main consequences of foreign interventions has been to fragment the sovereignty of the state and to dilute its responsibility by dissociating those who apply economic policy from those who are formally held responsible to society as a whole.

The privatization of power

The erosion of a government's administrative capacity brings in its train the delegitimation of public authority, a precursor to its confiscation by private actors. The venality of some civil servants weakens the capacity and the legitimacy of the state in general. At the same time, the inefficiency of all government caused by the loss of any central control of its powers and regulatory mechanisms favours opportunities for discretionary intervention and paralyses the implementation of reforms. This tendency is accentuated by an international context in which public agencies are being disempowered generally, largely as a result of economic and financial deregulation, and which is characterized by rapid capital movements, monetary instability, the apparent impotence of central banks, and similar factors.

Ever since the start of the colonial period, access to the state has been turned more or less into a source of private benefit. Today, the simultaneous erosion of government and the delegitimation of public authority have led further, to the confiscation of power by private actors.

The disorganized or even anarchic condition of public administration is conducive to the development of informal networks. These in turn become a means by which public authority, in fact lying in private hands, is actually exercised. This then emphasizes those aspects of the state which can be described as existing in a shadow world. At every level and in every sector, this mode of operation in parallel is acquiring ever more durable roots. Even the largest foreign companies are these days obliged, in a country like Cameroon, to do business in some obscure byways.

The end result is the emergence of a parallel government, but without the official or formal government ceasing to exist. In fact, this element of duality has become an integral part of the system. Thus, businesses which wish to change their official operating agreement[5] or any other basic document are obliged to negotiate in two areas at the same time. The official negotiations appear to be pure form and lead to no concrete result. The parallel negotiations, if suitable payment is made, are those which bring results. However, it is quite unthinkable to negotiate in the informal sphere alone, and not only because of the interest taken by the donor community. Matters have to be dealt with over the full spectrum of activity, and both formal and informal negotiations are organically linked to each other.

The vicious circle which such a situation represents is clear. On the one hand, nothing can be taken for granted; everything is liable for renegotiation in a parallel circuit. On the other hand, the growing frag-

---

[5] This is an agreement *('convention d'établissement')* negotiated between a company and the state, concerning payment of tax, customs dues, etc. Such accords are generally not made public.

mentation of government, which has gone so far as to result in the creation of a multiplicity of administrative fiefdoms, and the loss of control of government by the centre, is fertile ground for the appearance of a multitude of parallel circuits which gradually escape the control of any single locus of political power. Everyone tries to build his or her own sphere of power, however large or small. The movements which stem from the erosion of government simply reinforce the complexity of this process.

In this sense too, foreign interventions have acted as a catalyst. There is no doubt whatever that the external role in this process has been involuntary, but it has been effective none the less. The application of the following three principles has had particularly perverse results:

1. *The primary concern of the IMF, and to a lesser extent also of the World Bank, remains the state of public finances.* It is largely to ensure that states whose administrative capacity is in rapid decline nevertheless collect a minimum level of tax revenue that the donor agencies have resorted to the creation of small cells, disconnected from the rest of the public service, as mentioned earlier. Moreover, there is a tendency, when a reform does not work in the way it was intended, for another to be proposed in its place. The resulting multiplication of reform measures, which is both cause and consequence of the tradition of evasion, resistance and subterfuge of African societies, simply clogs the administrative apparatus still more, preventing any improved performance by its financial organs.

The unending quest to satisfy the donors' financial requirements has particularly pernicious consequences. Since the survival of a government depends increasingly on its external resources, it is increasingly led to concern itself more with its exterior respectability than its interior legitimacy. The public administration finds itself marginalized since, on the one hand, the government has to deal with demands from its foreign partners which are increasingly radical and detailed on matters of financial administration and economic arbitration, while, on the other hand, it must concentrate its attention on the small decision-making cells, leaving the rest of the civil service to continue in its path of ineffectiveness. The supremacy of external over internal legitimacy hastens the process of splintering, serves as a justification for the growth of shadow economic networks and leads to the passage of power into private hands generally, including in regard to the most basic public services.

2. In fact, *a second principle of structural adjustment programmes is the partial privatization of certain public services.* This has became increasingly necessary in Africa because of the financial difficulties which governments face and the widespread aversion to paying taxes. The proposal most commonly encountered is that of privatizing the

customs and their administration, theoretically for a temporary period only, by placing them in the hands of supervisory agencies such as the Société générale de surveillance (SGS), Veritas or Cotecna. In the countries with the most serious problems, even the administration of the public finances is indirectly privatized owing to the reliance on just one or two major foreign companies or agencies paying a minimum level of income to the state. In Liberia, for example, this role devolves on the maritime bureau which administers the registration of merchant ships under the Liberian flag and is administered by Americans, while in Equatorial Guinea such a role was played by the logging sector until the emergence of an oil industry.

It should be said that no part of what was intended by such measures has been achieved. The different actors concerned, notably customs officers and importers, resist such privatized customs supervision, and evasion is systematic. In Cameroon, for example, the privatization of the customs administration led to a fall in customs receipts because it caused a displacement of trade to Malabo in Equatorial Guinea and the unloading of cargoes outside normal working hours. In any case, private companies which are charged with performing a public service do not escape the entanglements of social and political life in the countries in which they operate. Inasmuch as the low level of tax recovery is essentially due to the existence of people enjoying exemption on political grounds, private agencies find themselves just as impotent as local civil servants, or even more so, when it comes to resisting political pressure. The substitution of foreign experts for local officials prevents African civil servants, as we may observe in Cameroon today, from benefiting from a hands-on learning process of good governance. On the contrary, by depriving local functionaries of their role, such a measure disposes them to resist. Overall, the increase in fiscal revenue created by such privatization measures seems to be exceptional rather than the general rule. The customs co-operation council of the European Union has demonstrated that, in the majority of African countries, the increase in income has not been sufficient to balance the costs of paying the administering agency, that exporters are subject to extra charges as a result of more frequent inspections, and that they pass these extra costs on to consumers. Furthermore, the strategy of delegating where possible encourages privatizations of the most crude sort. In Cameroon, the ports, or certain parts of them, have been quite simply turned into private operations by foreign traders, mostly Malaysian and Thai, with the active complicity of a few well-placed Cameroonians. Neither the customs service nor the SGS is authorized to set foot in these zones, still less to verify what takes place there.

Even the partial privatization of public services is a worrying development inasmuch as it alienates the sovereignty of the state. The consequences of this alienation can be serious. In political terms, it can lead to the rise of xenophobia. In economic terms, it can lead to the growing impossibility of reforming systems of government and economy. It is all the more dangerous in that the alienation of sovereignty extends itself to other sectors in various forms, because of the increasingly pervasive influence of the aid donors. Conditions are applied to the tax and fiscal regime, which lies at the heart of the definition of the functions of a state, and increasingly stringent conditions are applied to the national budget, with ever greater oversight of their implementation. This conditionality reflects a very specific view of what the organization of public life is or should be, namely that of the minimalist state.

3. *The third principle is that of the promotion of associations and other non-governmental organizations (NGOs)*, which are held to be representative of civil society. A careful analysis of the external finance which is transmitted through such NGOs, however, demonstrates that African actors use them in a particularly original way, which is frequently radically different from their official purpose. In general, what is taking place is a privatization of development. The concept of civil society, difficult to define at the best of times, becomes infinitely manipulable. The promotion of NGOs leads to an erosion of official administrative and institutional capacity, a reinforcement of the power of elites, particularly at the local level, or of certain factions, and sometimes a stronger ethnic character in the destination of flows of finance from abroad. In many cases, these NGOs are established by politicians, at national or local level, with a view to capturing external resources which henceforth pass through these channels on a massive scale. The phenomenon is particularly marked in countries in a state of civil war, such as in Liberia, where NGOs were set up by warring factions. But it also exists in countries where peace prevails. Since aid donors insist that ordinary people should be associated with development projects, fictional bodies are created headed by front-men or front-women appointed by the local government, such as the district health authorities in Cameroon. NGOs are frequently emanations of political parties, with most women's NGOs in Cameroon being connected to the women's league of the ruling party, the Cameroonian People's Democratic Movement. Development projects are used to favour certain groups whom those in power want to conciliate, such as minorities of Asian or Arab origin in Tanzania, and their international allies.

In fact, as the populations concerned realize perfectly well, such NGOs no longer have anything to do with civil society but represent simply the privatization of funds for aid and development. In an investigation published by one Cameroonian newspaper, NGOs were described by those interviewed as 'associations for squeezing the purse of the West', 'the latest Cameroonian discovery ... for getting access to credit', 'front companies for businessmen and politicians in particular', or 'passports or devices which allow smart people to embezzle money and to complicate things for real associations and NGOs' (*Dikalo*, 27 June–4 July 1996).

The abuse of NGOs is also clear from an examination of their activities. In some franc-zone countries, such as Senegal, Burkina Faso and Cameroon, NGOs are often among the leading smuggling organizations. Benefiting from the privileged status which allows them to import goods free of customs dues, some of them organize systematic smuggling rackets. In countries at war, such as Liberia, smuggling can even be in goods which are themselves illegal.

The unwitting contribution of aid donors to the further erosion of government administrative capacity and to the privatization of government services and public authority is all the more dramatic in the absence of checks and balances, or at least their extreme inadequacy. As we have noted, since the start of the colonial period access to the administration and to public authority in general has in effect been transformed into an instrument for the maintenance of private advantage, notably through such intermediaries as chiefs and interpreters. The novelty of the current process of privatization consists partly in the extension of this phenomenon to every level and branch of government, and in the impulse it gives to the breakdown of public administration and to the creation of ties between tenure of political power and economic crime. The privatization and the criminalization of the bureaucratic apparatus may be illustrated in three fields, which we shall examine next.

Privatization is permitted in fields as vital and fundamental for the state as security and the administration of the budget. Hence there is a development, in many countries south of the Sahara, of private police forces. A state which thus acquiesces in the renunciation of its claim to uphold a monopoly of legitimate violence opens the way to the privatization of violence and the loss of legitimacy of the public order. When the government is prepared to tolerate, as it does in Cameroon and to some extent in Côte d'Ivoire, a practice whereby civil servants must pay to receive their salaries and even a minister must pay for access to the budget allocated to his department, it is no longer accurate to speak of simple cases of corruption but rather of the privatization of public services. The same is true for those so-called traditional chiefs who continue to collect taxes even when these have been abolished by vote of parliament.

The struggle against economic crime is, in all African countries, no more than a pretence. It is handicapped by the inability of different branches of the administration to act in concert and by the confiscation of public powers by private persons. Sometimes this is to the advantage of leading public figures who are implicated, directly or via nominees, in illegal activity. At the same time, the fight against crime is ineffective because only the actual bandits are the subject of pursuit, and never those who protect them. It is known that special anti-corruption units and commissions exist essentially to attack political and economic rivals, while at the same time placating aid donors. In the Central African Republic, for example, the Anti-Corruption Commission created in 1994 was headed by a person – Jean-Jacques Demafouth – who was himself wanted for questioning by the French police, among other things for financial fraud and corruption.

Finally, justice itself is not immune from the erosion of government and from systematic corruption. In many cases, there is simply never any recourse to the judicial authorities. It is salutary to compare the number of scandals which are exposed every day in the press and that of the inquiries established into allegations of corruption, embezzlement or smuggling. In Cameroon, the phenomenon of the Feymen (see Box pp. 104–5) has never, at least at the time of writing, given rise to any conviction or even the opening of any formal inquiry. Not only is impunity almost total but it is not unusual to see incipient punishment transformed into a sideways promotion. Thus, before he was appointed Minister of Finance in Cameroon, one senior official had been responsible for the embezzlement of substantial sums of money in his previous function. In the Central African Republic, a paymaster-general who had diverted treasury funds was later promoted to the post of presidential aide with cabinet rank.

When there is recourse to the machinery of justice, it does not generally lead to any more satisfactory result. In countries such as Mozambique, Cameroon, Senegal or Côte d'Ivoire, the amount of a bribe to be paid is known, and is on a sliding scale according to the importance of the interests involved. The person with the most influence or who shows the greatest generosity wins a legal case. It is not unusual to see banks convicted when it was their clients who had committed an offence, as happened to the Société générale de banques de Côte d'Ivoire (SGBCI) or the BIAO, or to see civil servants penalized for having done their job too thoroughly, as has happened in Kenya and Senegal. This situation has made banks extremely cautious. What, in such circumstances, is the value of deposits, guarantees, capital assets or mortgages? The climate of total impunity is one of the leading stimuli to the proliferation of economic crime.

Contrary to what aid donors had intended, neither administrative nor economic reforms have halted the tendency for illegal forms of activity, or at least activites marginal to the rule of law, to grow. Such activities have been integrated into the mode of government which has been called *la politique du ventre*, and have become part of the development of new models of delinquent behaviour. Many examples show that this growth of illegality takes the form not so much of 'infringements of property' but of 'infringements of rights', to quote Michel Foucault.[6] In short, economic delinquency is overwhelmingly due not to the activities of insignificant individuals, of the common people, but of the most powerful people in society, the ruling classes, in pursuit of their political and economic goals. These powerful groups reserve to themselves, with complete impunity, 'the possibility of disobeying their own rules and their own laws' and of creating 'a vast economic sector' which lies outside the law.

The great deception and the economics of dirty tricks

The appropriation of the economic reforms which have been applied in recent years takes the form of the development of activities marginal to the legal and official corpus and the slow, ineluctable processes of administrative sclerosis and the privatization of government. This does not, however, condemn Africa inevitably to economic decline and a future in which crime reigns supreme. One observation which can be made on the basis of our discussion thus far concerns the ambiguity of economic configurations and the existence of a state of affairs far more complex than would be the case if the continent were wholly in the power of major criminal organizations.

It is true that Africa remains economically unproductive and that the pursuit of rents or unearned fees is becoming ever more extensive. There is a development of activities and financial flows considered by the international community to be improper or even criminal in nature. It is also the case that the mode of government which we have called *la politique du ventre* is becoming ever more predatory and that political elites are increasingly implicated in unsavoury activities. The creation of semi-clandestine forms of economic, financial and political power which shadow their official twins is becoming systematic. Violence is more frequent, including as an instrument in the management of economic resources. There is no denying that situations of war or anarchy are increasing.

But, at the same time, all of these developments are not merely other names for economic recession and the growth of crime. There are in fact few thoroughgoing criminal states in Africa. The development of illicit

---

[6] See P. Lascoumes, 'Michel Foucault et la délinquance des classes dirigeantes', *Le Monde*, 4 November 1995.

activity does not preclude economic growth, such as the 6 per cent growth in Mozambique in 1994. War and anarchy do not only have destabilizing effects; sometimes they may serve to stimulate economic and financial activity in neighbouring countries. Thus, a significant part of the economic dynamism of Côte d'Ivoire is attributable to revenues derived from the wars in Sierra Leone and, more particularly, Liberia (trades in hardwood, drugs, weapons, smuggled goods, stolen cars, gold, diamonds and rubber) and from local management of the economic affairs of UNITA, the Angolan movement which uses Abidjan as a rear base, including for its diamond business. The extension of forms of behaviour which are at or beyond the bounds of legality cannot simply be interpreted as a reflection of a fall in general moral standards. Ethical values and moral judgements are astonishingly ambivalent. All over Africa, the so-called 'dinosaurs' who hold power are also models of successful personal enterprise and the very epitome of witches. The legitimation of illicit activity by people at all social levels, by recourse to arguments such as that it creates jobs and wealth, and that it is often the only way of getting ahead, goes hand in hand with the widespread popular condemnation of existing governments. It could be said that the wealth of those in power is no more legitimate than that generated by the cocaine trade or any other activity which is regarded by the international community as criminal in nature. Surrounded by games of chance, financial trickery and frauds of all descriptions, the mood of the general population swings between one of mistrust (in wondering, for example, how games like Bindo and Panier de la Ménagère (see Box, pp. 104–5) actually work), and admiration, such as for the Feymen, who are widely admired and imitated. The connection between activities of this sort and political power is perceived as both positive and negative. Examples of the former include the popular belief that the organizers of the Zaïrean pyramid saving racket called Bindo were motivated by social concern: Bindo himself was often nicknamed 'the Saviour', 'the Messiah', 'the miracle man' and so on, while Feymen are often reputed to swindle the rich for the most part. Examples of a negative view of these practices may be seen in the rumours which circulate about who is really behind such rackets, who is manipulating them and profiting from them. There are constant political rumours, such as that Bindomania was created by President Mobutu as an outlet for political tensions, that the Feymen were protected by Jean Fochivé, former head of the Cameroonian security service, and so on.

Moreover, the aid donors, so concerned about the morality of governance, themselves find it difficult to reach a really clear position. They have no particular observation to make when fines for customs fraud or taxes are paid to a customs service in cash and with money derived from criminal activities or when finance ministries welcome with open

Some tricks of the trade

'419' frauds, so called from the article of the British colonial penal code which they contravene, or advance-fee frauds, flourish in Nigeria especially. The following page (p. 106) is a reproduction of a typical case. Generally, the fraud begins with a letter addressed to a private person or a company in the West, purporting to be from a group of employees of a parastatal company who are seeking to transfer money abroad. They propose, in return for a handsome share of the profits of the operation (often 30 to 50 per cent), to use the bank account of their foreign correspondent. The latter is thus asked to supply the number of his bank account, the bank details, some letterheads and a specimen signature. All of these are then used to empty the bank account in question. A variant form consists in persuading a rich foreigner who has shown some interest in the initial inquiry to come to Lagos in person. Once he is there, the organizers of the scheme use his credit card to empty his bank account. Recently, a new form of 419 has made its appearance. The organizers promise to hand over large sums in cash, in preparation for which a small advance payment needs to be made to cover the expenses of the transaction. The victim is eventually paid in counterfeit banknotes or gets nothing at all. One example provides a particularly good illustration of the imagination and the cynicism of those who operate these frauds. In recent months foreign businessmen have been approached with a proposal that they pay money in advance to facilitate the shipment and customs clearance of cargoes of toxic waste. These frauds have become so commonplace that the UK's Scotland Yard has set up a special unit to deal with them. Western police services have evidence that they are organized by highly organized gangs or guilds whose members are absolutely unscrupulous (some foreigners who have gone to Lagos to recover their assets have been murdered), and enjoy the active or passive complicity of public officials. The ring-leaders of '419' gangs enjoy excellent political protection and none of them has ever been extradited or convicted. The persistence and the scale of these frauds and the impunity of their authors lead observers to suppose that they benefit

arms investment funds from the most dubious sources. In an environment starved of investment there seems to be a general consensus that it is better to recycle dirty money than to attract no money at all.

The fundamental ambiguity of the frontiers between the legal and the illegal, the formal and the criminal, precludes too rigid or unequiv-

from collusion with people in power and that the military government is directly involved at a high level.

Bindo, so-called from the name of the 'conjuror' Bindo Bolembe, was a game of chance much in vogue in Zaïre in 1990–1. The individual gambler paid a certain amount of money and, after a month and a half, received a prize, such as a television, an electric cooker, or some similar reward. It seems to have started as a commercial venture designed to dispose of stocks of goods as quickly as possible. But the game soon acquired many imitators and rapidly degenerated into pure speculation, at which point it was in fact just another form of advance-fee fraud. The inevitable crash occurred when two generals highly placed in government, Generals Baramoto and Bolozi, withdrew from the Panier de la Ménagère ('The housewife's breadbasket'), an imitation of Bindo, with a profit of 27 billion zaïres. Their withdrawal then set off the riots and the wave of looting of September 1991.

Feymen are Cameroonian confidence tricksters who have operated, and perhaps are still operating, in Cameroon and in other African countries including Angola, Benin and South Africa, but also in Saudi Arabia, Yemen and Indonesia, for example. The word, in pidgin English, is evocative of the ability to acquire great wealth by witchcraft and by use of a diabolical intelligence, to be able to change into an animal or otherwise to change one's appearance, and to have the ability to become invisible. In general, Feymen organize confidence tricks, frauds and financial deceptions. Their hallmark is to eschew the use of violence, and to achieve their ends by pure deception. Feymen persuade their victims that they are being offered fabulous bargains. They are adept at selling goods which do not in fact exist, and at proposing non-existent projects to development and aid agencies so as to defraud foreign embassies. There are cases of some who claim to be the King of Cameroon. Others claim to be able to multiply banknotes. Although the impact of these practices on the economy is insignificant, their symbolic and moral effect is profound. The Feymen have become widely admired models for the young, among whom trickery is seen as a noble form of activity and deception, a national sport.

ocal a judgement about the current situation of Africa's economies. It is probably better to interpret them less in terms of a tendency to criminalization *per se* than in terms of the widespread use of deception and 'dirty tricks', represented by games of chance, pyramid schemes and other adventures as much as by the use of violence for economic ends.

From the desk of: DR. M.

CONFIDENTIAL

ACCOUNT'S DEPARTMENT

FEDERAL MINISTRY OF PETROLEUM RESOURCES,
IKOYI, LAGOS, NIGERIA.

RESIDENTIAL ADDRESS:
GOVERNMENT QUARTERS,
5, SHODIPO STREET,
PAPA - ASHAFA, AGEGE,
LAGOS, NIGERIA.

ATTENTION: *MR.*

11TH FEBRUARY, 1997

RE: A LETTER SEEKING FOR YOUR MUTUAL CO-OPERATION AND ASSISTANCE IN A U.S.
$32.5 MILLION BUSINESS TRANSACTION

WITH UTMOST RESPECT TO YOUR HIGH HONOUR, I AM **DR. MICHAEL SEGUN SMITH,** A SENIOR
ACCOUNTANT IN THE FEDERAL MINISTRY OF PETROLEUM RESOURCES IN THE COUNTRY.
CONSEQUENT UPON INFORMATION GATHERED ON YOU FROM A RELIABLE AND RESPECTED FRIEND
OF MINE [A FORMER DIPLOMAT] WHO ONCE SERVED IN A DIPLOMATIC MISSION IN YOUR
COUNTRY. SHE ASSURED US THAT YOU ARE CAPABLE AND RELIABLE TO TRANSACT THIS
BUSINESS WITH US WITHOUT REGRETING OF WHICH WE WOULD LIKE YOU TO TREAT THIS
TRANSACTION WITH UTMOST SENSE OF MATURITY, CONFIDENTIALITY AND URGENCY, SO AS
TO AVOID EXPOSURE AND TO PROTECT OUR GOOD NAMES AND POSITIONS IN THE MINISTRY
AS WELL AS IN BOTH COUNTRIES.

I THEREFORE WISH TO INTIMATE YOU OF A CONTRACT TRANSACTION INVOLVING THE ABOVE
STATED SUM AND HOPE THAT YOU WILL BE INTERESTED TO ASSIST AND CO-OPERATE WITH
US IN THIS TRANSACTION THAT WILL BENEFIT BOTH OF US IMMEDIATELY WHEN SUCCESSFULLY
EXECUTED. BEEN THE SENIOR ACCOUNTANT IN THE MINISTRY, I APPROVE AND HASTEN PAY-
MENT FOR OUTSTANDING DEBTS AND FINANCIAL OBLIGATIONS OF THE MINISTRY. I. AM
PRESENTLY IN THE PROCESS OF APPROVING PAYMENT FOR A CONTRACT AWARDED BY MY
COLLEAGUES IN THIS TRANSACTION, [THE CONTRACT AWARDING OFFICERS IN THE MINISTRY].
THE CONTRACT WAS AWARDED SOME YEARS BACK TO SOME EXPERTRIATES IN THE COUNTRY, BUT
WAS OVER-VALUED TO THE TUNE OF U.S.$32,500.000.00 [THIRTY TWO MILLION, FIVE
HUNDRED THOUSAND UNITED STATES DOLLARS]. THE AMOUNT IS NOW FLOATING.

I AND MY COLLEAGUES [THE CONTRACT AWARDING OFFICERS] WITH THE ASSISTANCE OF TOP
OFFICIALS OF THE CENTRAL BANK OF NIGERIA ARE SERIOUSLY WORKING IN CONCERT TO
TRANSFER THE MONEY INTO A FOREIGN ACCOUNT, AND ALSO SEEK YOUR ASSISTANCE AND
PERMISSION TO EITHER RECEIVE THE MONEY INTO YOUR ACCOUNT OR FOR YOU TO VISIT US IN
THE COUNTRY SO AS TO SEE THE MONEY AND ASSIST US IN SECRETLY MOVING OUT THE MONEY
INTO A FOREIGN ACCOUNT. YOUR COMMISSION WILL BE 25% OF THE TOTAL SUM AND YOU MUST
DEDUCT YOUR PERCENTAGE IMMEDIATELY THE MONEY GOT INTO THE FOREIGN ACCOUNT, 5% WILL
OFFSET OUR EXPENSES AND 70% WILL BE FOR ME AND THE REST OF MY COLLEAGUES IN THIS
DEAL HERE IN NIGERIA.

ALL NECESSARY MODALITIES HAVE BEEN PROPERLY WORKED OUT WITH THE OFFICIALS OF THE
FEDERAL MINISTRY OF FINANCE AND THE CENTRAL BANK OF NIGERIA TO ENSURE A HITCH-FREE
REMITTANCE OF THIS FUND INTO YOUR ACCOUNT WITHOUT PROBLEM IF YOU PERMIT US. AS
SOON AS I RECEIVE YOUR POSITIVE AND IMMEDIATE REPLY WHICH YOU MUST SEND THROUGH
"DHL" COURIER SERVICE TO ME AT MY ABOVE RESIDENTIAL ADDRESS [ONLY], FURTHER
DETAILS REGARDING THE TRANSACTION WILL BE FAXED TO YOU IMMEDIATELY WITHOUT DELAY.
FOR SECURITY REASONS, DO **NOT** MENTION MONEY IN YOUR REPLY, SIMPLY REFER TO THIS
CODE: "MUCOOP - ANASINMOBT". YOUR SHOULD INCLUDE YOUR HOME & OFFICE PHONE & FAX
NUMBERS WHERE YOU COULD BE CONTACTED FOR FURTHER COMMUNICATIONS AND ALSO INDICATE
YOUR INTEREST AND ABILITY TO CO-OPERATE WITH US IN THIS REGARD. WE ARE HEREBY
ASSURING YOU THAT THIS BUSINESS IS 100% RISK-FREE GUARANTEED.

PLEASE IT IS **VERY IMPORTANT** TO SEND YOUR FIRST [POSITIVE] REPLY THROUGH MY ABOVE
RESIDENTIAL ADDRESS [ONLY] **STRICTLY** BY **DHL COURIER SERVICE ONLY.** WHILE FURTHER
COMMUNICATIONS SHALL BE BY FAX TO AVOID EXPOSURE AND FOR SECURITY REASONS.
PLEASE TAKE NOTE WHETHER ON DEMAND OR NOT, DO **NOT** FAX OR POST BACK THIS MY LETTER
OF PROPOSAL TO ANYBODY OR GROUP IN MY COUNTRY [EVEN MYSELF] TO ENSURE ADEQUATE
SECURITY AND SAFETY TRANSACTION.

ANTICIPATING YOUR CO-OPERATION AND IMMEDIATE RESPONSE.

YOURS FAITHFULLY,

Figure 4.1   An example of '419'

The great deception

Forged documents and forgeries of all descriptions are, so to speak, common currency. In recent years the explosion of forged documents has been staggering. It is no longer possible to calculate the scale of the use of forged medical drugs, known as 'back garden pharmacy' ('pharmacie de gazon') in Cameroon, or 'open air pharmacy' *('pharmacie par terre')* in Côte d'Ivoire. In France, an inquiry was recently launched into responsibility for the distribution of false vaccines during a meningitis epidemic in Niger in 1995, as a result of which it has already come to light that the Nigerian government distributed pirated products in the guise of aid. In Cameroon, a study by the organization Pharmaciens sans frontières has calculated that more than 60 per cent of the national market in medical drugs is taken by pirated drugs manufactured in Nigeria, India or Thailand, but also manufactured in the country itself, sometimes, for example, by filling capsules with ordinary flour. In Côte d'Ivoire, so-called 'Chinese medicine' is sold in street markets alongside drugs stolen from hospitals, drugs which have passed their sell-by dates and which have been smuggled into the country, and simple imitation drugs and false vaccines. In the Democratic Republic of Congo, the Lufu market has been nicknamed the 'illness and death market' on account of the vast quantity of medical drugs and other products which have been damaged or have passed their sell-by date but which are to be found on sale.

There are pirated drinks, such as wine made with industrial alcohol, on sale in Cameroon, false fertilizer and false insecticides which are in fact flour dyed pink, sold especially in the north of Cameroon, where the SODECOTON company is based. There is pirated salt, in fact salt of poor quality imported from Iran and bagged by a public company, Selcam. The Feymen have even managed the most breathtaking deception of all – the open sale of objects which have no use or purpose whatsoever.

False documents are a Nigerian speciality, although forgeries are to be found throughout Africa, in such quantity that banks will no longer accept property title deeds as loan guarantees, while European immigration services routinely suspect African passports of being forged, including (or perhaps especially) diplomatic passports. The Cameroonian authorities recently declared that they had dismantled a forgery ring, composed of employees of the airline Camair, which specialized in printing false air tickets. The company is estimated to have lost more than CFA 100 million as a result of the activities of this gang. In Mozambique, Côte d'Ivoire, Senegal and Benin, among many other countries, any document imaginable can be bought, including false immigration documents, false health or sickness certificates, false official texts or laws, false driving licences, false certificates stating that the bearer is not HIV-positive, and many more. In the Central African Republic, forged official documents and forged treasury bills have been used to embezzle very large sums of money.

Even the means of production can be forged or falsified. There are cases of fishermen simply pouring pesticide into water and hauling in the dead fish which float to the surface, which can then be marketed.

The principle of forgery and deception extends to interpersonal relations and most particularly to monetary transactions. The proliferation of forged banknotes, particularly in Central Africa, can be interpreted as the revival or continuation of a long tradition. History records that, as early as the fifteenth century, the region was using numerous different currencies, both real and forged, often introduced by foreign traders seeking to derive the maximum margin of profit from their business dealings in Africa. These days, however, the traffic in counterfeit currency is more often organized by African elites. In 1994, President Mobutu of Zaïre organized the smuggling of officially sanctioned counterfeit banknotes via a number of his Lebanese business associates, such as the Skydec company affiliated with Diamco, or via Israeli business acquaintances. Fifteen tonnes of new zaïre banknotes printed in Europe and fifteen tonnes printed in Argentina were loaded into the security vehicles of the central bank, but without this institution having any control over the process. The President was able to choose whether to change some of these banknotes into dollars or to use them for paying the army. In Kenya, President arap Moi has also used the same technique of commissioning official counterfeit banknotes. Although these were never registered by the central bank, they were used for fraud on a massive scale and for paying the expenses of an election campaign. In Nigeria, routes for the smuggling of counterfeit currency are largely controlled by Ibo drug-trafficking gangs. Whole containerloads of forged banknotes are imported from Korea and Taiwan. Forged notes also circulate in the franc zone, notably through a traffic in forged CFA notes and forged dollar bills in Cameroon and Equatorial Guinea.

In all these countries, police officers organize unofficial roadblocks or claim to have witnessed non-existent offences as a pretext for extorting bribes. In Cameroon, Senegal and Côte d'Ivoire, false experts offer their services to evaluate the price of goods such as cars and telephone equipment which are sold when government departments are being re-equipped or reorganized.

Most statistics are false. In Cameroon for example, according to different sources and in various circumstances, the population of Douala is estimated at 800,000, 1.2 million, or 2 million people. In most countries, the precise number of civil servants is unknown. In 1990, 16,000 civil servants were removed from the official payroll in Tanzania. In

Guinea, 143 officials were recently asked to verify the lists of civil servants with a view to removing the names of non-existent people. In Côte d'Ivoire, there are so many phantom public employees that it was found necessary to carry out a full identification costing more than CFA 170 million. In Cameroon, no civil servants have been officially recruited since 1987, but it is possible to identify no less than 20,000 officials recruited since that date.

Accounts can be falsified, particularly when it is necessary to react to pressure from donors and to the imposition of conditionality. The BCCI affair revealed that some commercial banks are prepared to act as the accomplices of governments in such acts of falsification, in return for future financial compensation or other advantage, thus allowing the host country continued access to loans from the international financial institutions. But the donor institutions themselves manipulate statistics for a similar reason, a specific demonstration being during the negotiation of structural adjustment loans in the franc zone following the devaluation of the CFA franc in January 1994. For a week, French and international civil servants were locked in discussion in an effort to identify the 'correct' figures which could be published in a study of the funds' flow account of the CFA states. Six months later, these figures were once more subject to negotiation.

These days, forgery and falsification of all types have become so elaborate that most reforms are false and the aid institutions themselves are caught up in the spiral of lies in proposing, for example, conditionalities which are intended only for public presentation. If one were to have serious regard for the quantitative and qualitative criteria which in theory constitute the various conditionalities, countries like the Democratic Republic of Congo, Cameroon, Congo-Brazzaville, Chad and Equatorial Guinea, as well as more respectable countries such as Senegal or Ghana, would fail to qualify for further assistance for structural adjustment, and in some cases this has been the case for years already.

The transparency which in some lights seems a characteristic of African societies, in which people quite often are willing to reveal more readily than elsewhere the existence of this or that subterfuge, is thus also a fiction. Things are known without being said, and any item of information is subject to invention. As is often said in Cameroon, 'that is not important. It is only words.'

It could be said, with reasonable accuracy, that the examples of falsification which we have listed could be found in every continent at almost any stage of its history. What is particular about African countries today is the systematic character of the process and the significance which may be attributed to it.

This question of the meaning of such falsification deserves to be considered at greater length. Not every allegation of forgery is necessarily well founded or true, and it is quite frequent for one or another entrepreneur to accuse a competitor of selling pirated goods in order to protect his own monopoly in a specific market, or to prevent or encourage imports, and so on. The truth or otherwise of such allegations is not the matter of most importance. Rather, the object of our attention should be the significance of a world largely dominated by myriad fictions. An accusation of drug smuggling reveals the apparent meaning of relationships which themselves come close to being based on a simple deception: it matters little if an individual – Moshood Abiola, say, or General Babangida – is really implicated in the drug trade, as is often alleged. The mere allegation reveals the way in which such people are regarded by the general public and, at the same time, reflects a common perception that the wealth of people in positions of power is by nature illegitimate. Make-believe ends up by becoming true and transforms the nature of perception by giving it a new sense. What is said about the economy has only slight importance since everyone can do the opposite of what he says.

But this everyone knows.

The economy of dirty tricks
Despite the ambivalence, flexibility and obliqueness of economic situations and meanings, an outgrowth of the social capital of African economies, it is incorrect to label the strategies of African states as being criminal in nature. However, it is reasonable to consider them in terms of 'dirty tricks' inasmuch as the acquisition of wealth does not take place in most cases according to conventional strategies, but via methods which involve a significant degree of fantasy, deception and coercion.

The use of violence as a means of acquiring wealth lies deep in Africa's historical experience. This tradition more or less disappeared after independence, but is today reappearing in spectacular fashion as a result of economic crisis, the collapse of public administration and the fragmentation of power. Testimony to this includes the insidious violence of witchcraft and the growth of witchcraft accusations on economic grounds, the practice of extortion by simple threat or brute force, and the levy of illegal taxes or similar impositions, including the use of roadblocks which are illegal but are organized by senior officials. To this list we may add the frequency with which goods are confiscated or monies embezzled, the plunder of natural resources including precious stones and hardwood, but also works of art, and advance sales of oil. All of these practices amount to the reworking, in new forms, of the operating methods used by the old concessionary companies, including the development of private militias and police forces and even a revival of slavery.

But the current situation also recalls another historical experience, namely, that of the accumulation of wealth by imaginative means. As

Filip de Boeck has demonstrated in regard to the diamond trade, money and material wealth generally have to be 'caught' or 'captured', like the quarry in a traditional hunt, by means of 'playing' (de Boeck, 1998). And, in fact, economic activities in contemporary Africa are often unpredictable, irrational and downright dangerous. African economies are characterized by their uncertainty, by the struggle for survival, and by the existence of powerful external constraints. An observer can hardly fail to be struck by the ubiquity of language and symbols drawn from the repertoire of games and tricks. This is symbolized, naturally enough, by the growth in the number of casinos and gambling or lottery schemes, and in the countries of the franc zone by the creation of local PMU systems for gambling on French horse races. But more original and no doubt more illuminating for analytical purposes is the regular appearance in recent years of more devious and deceptive schemes which are certainly criminal at least in part, but which are also partly games of chance, such as the infamous '419' rackets in Nigeria, Bindo in Zaïre, and the tricks operated by Feymen in Cameroon.

As we have seen, the use of violence and deception for economic purposes is more than simply a practice consequent upon the weakening of the state, symbolized by its loss of the monopoly of legitimate violence. Naturally enough, insecurity, banditry and economic violence are particularly in evidence when the political situation is confused, or when foreign actors take a major share in the management of a national economy, for example, in Sierra Leone, Liberia, Tanzania and Cameroon, where the presence of strangers has certainly increased the potential for violence. But it is always the power-holders who are at the centre of such a train of events. In Tanzania, it is the so-called 'container bourgeoisie' which organizes the plunder of natural and mineral resources, in collaboration with Thai businessmen. In Cameroon, it is the clique around President Biya which is the architect of the plunder of the forests.

Violence and deception are used, above all, to control resources and to dominate society at large or those of its members who produce and reproduce capital. By heightening the general feeling of insecurity, violence intensifies the need for all of these to seek the protection, even in a privatized form, of those who wield economic and political power. In this way, it reinforces the tendency to clientelism, co-optation and collaboration. As Kopytoff (1987b) has suggested, the prolonged use of violence is not necessarily antithetical to the consolidation of power. African societies can co-exist with a certain degree of public disorder, and this co-existence has in fact been a constant in African history, both before and since the colonial period. The consolidation of power has taken place in African countries not as a result of the abolition of conflicts and violence but by the recognition and control of these conflicts by the central government. All the acts of deception and all the confidence tricks which we have described could be less ephemeral than they may appear. Casinos are known as places for laundering dirty money, as in South Africa, Namibia, Gabon, Cameroon, Côte d'Ivoire and Senegal. The same is true for national gambling schemes and lotteries, such as the Socajeux in the Central African Republic which is connected to the milieu of organized crime in Taiwan. It is also true of the Feymen, behind whose confidence tricks it is possible to identify networks for money-laundering and trafficking in counterfeit banknotes and possibly narcotics. The connection between different sorts of illicit activity is often very explicit. '419' frauds, for example, actually flaunt the illicit aspect of the operation which they propose as bait for their victims. In the proposal letters which are the starting-point of these frauds, there is explicit mention of the dumping of toxic waste, of funds corruptly acquired, and of the illegal evasion of currency controls.

But horse-racing schemes, lotteries, '419' and Bindo represent only a tiny part of the tendency to engage in economic games of chance or to gamble on evading economic controls. In Nigeria, for example, the drug trade is viewed as essentially a game of chance. Experiences in activities of this sort are the symbol of a specific and systematic way of thinking about money and economics, which does not necessarily exclude other ways. In this approach the element of chance appears to be of overwhelming importance in situations of disorder. This condition of disarray is characterized by an over-esteem for financial success and by a purely financial concept of the meaning of money and wealth. Money is seen as something having a magical and mysterious quality, which bears no relation to work and effort. Speaking very generally, there is a propensity to transform words, written and spoken, into money. The ability to make a show of respecting donor conditionalities while flouting them directly, and the eagerness to adopt whatever idea is currently in vogue among the donors, such as the creation of a Ministry for Regional Integration in Senegal in the late 1980s, the creation of ministries for women almost everywhere, the establishment of agencies to consider the problems of the environment, the promotion of NGOs, and the issuing of decentralization laws and such like, are all examples of another form of game or fantasy. Contrary to what has often been believed, and to borrow the title of a book by Jane Guyer (1995), money matters in Africa. The quest for money and wealth is organized in ways which are original and in part according to the mode of games of chance.

Violence and game-playing appear increasingly important in the way in which the economy is regulated in modern Africa. The organizers or manipulators of violence and deception are also the main mediators of economic activity. Their aim is to obtain simultaneous monopolies of economic and socio-political life, in extremely unstable situations. It is impossible not to be struck by the fact that these people are the very same individuals as those who hold power, and by the small size of the elites. Equally striking is the precarious nature of social and economic mobility. This is, although in part only, linked to the very ambiguity of violence and of deception considered as economic instruments. These are double-edged weapons, since they guarantee success against rivals who cannot use the same instruments but they also open the field to the rise of potential new players, making use of the same means, which are so terribly effective, of economic competition.

The popular support which elites, for good or ill, were able to obtain in the past by the distribution of jobs in public employment, the awarding of special exemptions and other advantages, such as import licences or privileged access to foreign exchange, has gradually evaporated under the combined effect of crisis and reform. This support they now have to obtain by new means of access to resources, economic and political. Today, the new means of control are often exercised indirectly, through protection and the use of tax and fiscal regulations, through illicit activities involving trickery, fraud and violence, by means of protection from or access to informal trade, and through games of chance.

Conclusion

JEAN-FRANÇOIS BAYART

There is a strong possibility that sub-Saharan Africa is returning to the 'heart of darkness'. This, we must repeat, is not synonymous with 'tradition' or 'primitiveness', but is related to the manner in which Africa is inserted in the international system through economies of extraction or predation in which many of the leading operators are foreigners, whose local African partners have to a considerable degree based their careers on the use of armed force. The relevance of Joseph Conrad's novel is clear for anyone who has an interest in situations like those of the Democratic Republic of Congo, Liberia, Sierra Leone, the Central African Republic, Sudan or Equatorial Guinea. Nevertheless, it would be wise to remain cautious in making use of the idea that we are witnessing a revival of some of the political and economic patterns of the nineteenth century. Naturally enough, there is a clear element of continuity inasmuch as the process of criminalization often expresses the maturation of a 'social capital' which has been built up over recent decades. This appears to come about when elements are activated which, in themselves, imply no pre-ordained direction or end use, but which, in the contemporary context, enable, facilitate or accelerate the fusion of criminal and political practices. The context in which this occurs is a modern one. It cannot be dissociated from the process of globalization of the planet, one of the key aspects of which is, at least for the time being, an unrestrained tendency towards economic and financial liberalization. Criminal organizations are certainly not slow to take advantage of this and to globalize or at least 'delocalize' their strategies. From this point of view, Africa's comparative advantage, although limited, is a substantial one. It is in any case such as to retain the attention of various sectors in the industrialized world, whose zeal for the continent sometimes gets the better of their disinterest. Congolese, with their habitual cynical humour, associate international co-operation with an act of theft. The phrase *'kosala cop'*, short for *'kosala coopération,* means 'to steal' in Lingala. Moreover, Africa's comparative advantage is such as to be of interest to criminal networks from around the world, including Corsican, Sicilian, Chinese, Lebanese, Russian, Ukrainian and Israeli gangsters or adventurers who crowd on to the airlines flying to Africa and there meet their counter-parts who are interested in the conquest of the most profitable markets of the developed economies, namely those in drugs, diamonds, illegal immigration, and high-value minerals.

More fundamentally, the lines of continuity or revival which impress themselves on the observer in fact represent at the same time a change of great importance in Africa. Without even stopping to dis-cuss the growth in Africa's population and the technological innova-tions which have transformed the way in which African societies are organized, we may consider the implications of the formation of cen-tralized and bureaucratically run states, a process in which war has, in a tragic number of cases, been a main catalyst, and the accumulation of capital, which helps to create real dominant classes who own the principal factors of production, notably land. While circumstances vary throughout the continent, it does appear that this change, begun in the 1930s in the neo-mercantilist mode, is continuing today through the political economies of predation and war. It is possible that this was already the underlying issue of the great upheavals of the nine-teenth century which were ended by colonization, or at least curtailed by it. The fact remains that the social groups which benefited from col-laboration with the European occupier, from nationalist mobilization, from the accession to independence, from nationalization of the econ-omy and then its liberalization, are today well placed to benefit from the eventual criminalization of the sub-continent. If they do this, it will be in the guise of multi-party politics, the restoration of authori-tarian government or armed conflict. Behind the tumult of events, what is taking place is the formation of systems of inequality whose base was created in most respects a half-century ago or, in some cases, long before that. If this hypothesis turns out to be correct, a whole series of false alternatives would cease to be applicable. Dissidence, war and banditry, the last a transnational activity *par excellence,* do not necessarily threaten the formation or existence of a state. They can, on the contrary, aid its centralization (Barkey, 1994). To quote an 'apocryphal saying of the Baluchis', quoted by Olivier Roy, 'the smug-gler has need of frontiers'.

Always under pressure to record short-term events, the media sometimes attach too much importance to ruptures which are more apparent than real. Is the political economy of war so very different from that of the regime which it destroys and sweeps away (Marchal and Messiant, 1997)? Does the logic of privatization really mark a break with that of public enterprises? Meanwhile, commentators tend to ignore some fundamental social changes. The criminalization of the state encompasses at least two of these: it contributes to a radical increase in the monetarization of societies, if only by promoting a conception of the search for money and wealth as activities analogous to hunting a wild animal, and this is accompanied by a general process of falsification. It also contributes to an unrestrained privatization not only of the productive sector of the economy, but also of sovereignty and of the sovereign functions of the state, such as the maintenance of customs barriers, the concession of territories or harbour enclaves to foreign entrepreneurs, the safeguarding of internal security and national defence, and of peacekeeping in general.

At bottom, the criminalization of politics is doubtless no more than a symptom of these deeper changes. It ushers in a period of history in which the mercenaries of Executive Outcomes, Asian timber merchants or the French and Israeli trainers of Presidential Guards are the anti-heroes, like the figure of Kurtz in *Heart of Darkness*, but not necessarily the leading figures. The elusiveness of Africa lies also in its refusal to be subject to statistics: 'when one has got to make the correct entries, one comes to hate those savages', laments a character in Conrad's novel, who nowadays would no doubt be working for the World Bank. Africa is resistant to every conditionality and its democratization remains a great leap into the unknown, considering the degree to which popular sovereignty is alienated and the systematic creation of shadow networks of power is being precipitated by the privatization of both the state and the economy. But Africa is busily recreating itself, and in this process crime is not shorn of all 'usefulness', as Marx recognized.

Just as in western Sicily the use of banditry by landlords seems to have been the means of accumulating land, and just as crime was a significant means for Italian, Jewish and Irish immigrants to gain access to the American dream, so has drug-trafficking become for African Americans living in inner-city ghettos what bootlegging was for others in the 1920s. Informal and illicit trade, financial fraud, the systematic evasion of rules and international agreements could turn out to be a means, among others, by which certain Africans manage to survive and to stake their place in the maelstrom of globalization. In the state of dependency in which Africa remains, *mètis* and *débrouillardise* are more than ever the qualities required of the pioneer, the spice of adventure. Some writings on surplus value (Marx quoted in Bottomore and Rubel, 1964: 158–60) which have been too easily set aside recall that crime, which is a distinctly relative phenomenon, can have productive consequences as great as those of strikes in the invention of capitalism, and that there would not be a world market, or nations, if counter-movements of this scale did not exist. Since the age of Adam, the tree of evil has also been the tree of knowledge.

On the origins of the state in Africa and on *la politique du ventre,* see J.-F. Bayart, *L'Etat en Afrique: la politique du ventre* (Fayard, Paris, 1989), translated into English as *The State in Africa: the politics of the belly* (Longman, London, 1993). This offers a synthesis covering most of sub-Saharan Africa but largely omitting South Africa, Ethiopia and Sudan.

On the political economy of the postcolonial state, the reader may consult B. Hibou, *L'Afrique est-elle protectionniste? Les chemins buis-sonniers de la libéralisation extérieure* (Karthala, Paris, 1996) and, from a more anthropological perspective, S. Berry, *No Condition is Permanent: the social dynamics of agrarian change in sub-Saharan Africa* (University of Wisconsin Press, Madison, WI, 1993); J. MacGaffey, *Entrepreneurs and Parasites: the struggle for indigenous capitalism in Zaïre* (Cambridge University Press, Cambridge, 1987) and in collaboration with others, *The Real Economy of Zaïre: the con-tribution of smuggling to national wealth* (James Currey, London, 1991). J.-L. Gombeaud, C. Moute and S. Smith have provided a remarkable journalistic study of cocoa marketing in Côte d'Ivoire in *La Guerre du cacao: histoire secrète d'un embargo* (Calmann-Lévy, Paris, 1990).

On Africa's crisis, see J. Coussy and J. Vallin (eds), *Crise et popula-tion en Afrique: crises économiques, politiques d'ajustement et dynamiques démographiques* (CEPED, Paris, 1996). On the origins and the failure of structural adjustment programmes, see G. Duruflé, *L'Ajustement structurel en Afrique (Sénégal, Côte-d'Ivoire, Madagascar)* (Karthala, Paris, 1988) and *Le Sénégal peut-il sortir de la crise? Douze ans d'ajustement structurel au Sénégal* (Karthala, Paris, 1994) as well as O. Vallée, *Le Prix de l'argent CFA: heurs et malheurs de la zone franc* (Karthala, Paris, 1989).

On the economic history which underlies postcolonial develop-ments, especially useful are R. Law (ed.), *From Slave Trade to*

'Legitimate' Commerce: the commercial transition in nineteenth century West Africa (Cambridge University Press, Cambridge, 1995); G. Clarence-Smith (ed.), The Economics of the Indian Ocean Slave Trade in the Nineteenth Century (Frank Cass, London, 1989); D.D. Cordell, Dar al-Kuti and the Last Years of the Trans-Saharan Slave Trade (University of Wisconsin Press, Madison, WI, 1985); J.J. Ewald, Soldiers, Traders and Slaves: state formation and economic transformation in the Greater Nile Valley, 1700–1885 (University of Wisconsin Press, Madison, WI, 1990); and the path-breaking work of J.C. Miller, Way of Death: merchant capitalism and the Angolan slave trade, 1730–1830 (University of Wisconsin Press, Madison, WI, 1988). On the sequence of events in colonial times and the logic of 'straddling' which developed at that time, see G. Kitching, Class and Economic Change in Kenya: the making of an African petite-bourgeoisie (Yale University Press, New Haven, CT, 1980).

The hypothesis of a criminalization of the state was mooted by J.-F. Bayart at the beginning of the 1990s in a number of essays: see 'L'afropessimisme par le bas', Politique africaine, 40 (December 1990) (reprinted in J.-F. Bayart, A. Mbembe, C. Toulabor, Le Politique par le bas en Afrique noire: contributions à une problématique de la démocratie (Karthala, Paris, 1992: 257–65); 'L'Etat' in C. Coulon and D. Martin (eds), Les Afriques politiques (La Découverte, Paris, 1991), pp. 213–30; 'Fin de partie au sud du Sahara? La politique africaine de la France' in S. Michailof (ed.), La France et l'Afrique: vade-mecum pour un nouveau voyage (Karthala, Paris, 1993), pp. 112–29; 'Conclusion' in P. Geschiere and P. Konings (eds), Itinéraires d'accumulation au Cameroun/Pathways to Accumulation in Cameroun (Karthala and Afrika-Studiecentrum, Paris and Leiden, 1993), pp. 335–44; 'Réflexions sur la politique africaine de la France', Politique africaine, 58 (June 1995), pp. 41–50; and in various articles and interviews in Le Nouvel Observateur, La Croix-L'Evénement, Jeune Afrique, and Marchés tropicaux et méditerranéens between 1990 and 1995.

The most searching case study to date is that by W. Reno on the 'shadow state': Corruption and State Politics in Sierra Leone (Cambridge University Press, Cambridge, 1995). On the 'strategies of tension' which underlie the process of restoration of authoritarian governments, see for example Africa Watch, Divide and Rule: sponsored ethnic violence in Kenya (Human Rights Watch, New York, 1993).

On the subject of war, several titles are distinguished by the quality of their analysis in a literature which is abundant but is too often either sensationalist or flawed by good intentions: C. Geffray, La Cause des armes au Mozambique: anthropologie d'une guerre civile (Karthala, Paris, 1990); S.E. Hutchinson, Nuer Dilemmas: coping with money, war and the state (University of California Press, Berkeley, CA, 1996); R. Marchal,

'Les *mooryann* de Mogadiscio: formes de la violence dans un espace urbain en guerre', *Cahiers d'études africaines*, 130, XXXIII-2 (1993), pp. 295–320, and, in collaboration with C. Messiant, *Les Chemins de la guerre et de la paix en Afrique* (Karthala, Paris, 1997); and P. Richards, *Fighting for the Rain Forest: war, youth and resources in Sierra Leone* (James Currey, Oxford, 1996). For a comparative approach to the relationship of war and criminalization, see M. van Creveld, *The Transformation of War* (The Free Press, New York, 1991) and P. Hassner, 'Par-delà la guerre et la paix: violence et intervention après la guerre froide', *Etudes* (September 1996), pp. 149–58.

Various criminal trades are unevenly documented. Other than the so-called 'confidential' newsletters, whose information must be regarded with caution *(La Lettre du continent, Nord–Sud Export, Africa Analysis, Africa Confidential)*, the following works may be consulted:

- on drug-trafficking, the various publications by the *Observatoire géopolitique des drogues*; the United States Department of State, Bureau for International Narcotics and Law Enforcement Affairs, *International Narcotics Control Strategy Report* (Washington DC, annual publication); E. Fottorino, *La Piste blanche: l'Afrique sous l'emprise de la drogue* (Balland, Paris, 1991); M. Cesoni, 'Les routes des drogues: explorations en Afrique sub-saharienne', *Revue Tiers monde*, 131 (July–September 1992).
- an exceptional example of an international criminal affair, with a great deal of information on Africa, is described in L. Gurwin and P. Truell, *False Profits: the inside story of BCCI, the world's most corrupt financial empire* (Houghton Mifflin and Co., Boston, MA, 1992), and *The BCCI Affair* (Report to the Committee on Foreign Relations, United States Senate, by Senator John Kerry and Senator Hank Brown, Washington DC, December 1992).
- on trafficking in works of art, see P.R. Schmidt and R.J. McIntosh (eds), *Plundering Africa's Past* (Indiana University Press and James Currey, Bloomington, IN and London, 1996).
- on the diamond trade, F. Misser and O. Vallée, *Les Gemmocraties: l'économie politique du diamant africain* (Desclée de Brouwer, Paris, 1997) and 'Les massacres de Katekelayi et de Luamuela (Kasai oriental)', *Politique africaine*, 6 (May 1982), pp. 72–106.
- on the liberalization and globalization of the trade in precious stones, see C.S.L. Chachage, 'The Meek Shall Inherit the Earth but not the Mining Rights: the mining industry and accumulation in Tanzania' in P. Gibbon (ed.), *Liberalised Development in Tanzania* (Nordiska Afrikainstitutet, Uppsala, 1995), pp. 37–108.
- on the criminalization of environmental networks, see S. Ellis, 'Of Elephants and Men: politics and nature conservation in South Africa', *Journal of Southern African Studies* 20 (1) (1994), pp. 53–70.

For studies of various unorthodox paths of social ascent, the reader may consult, other than the works of J. MacGaffey cited above, L. White, *The Comforts of Home: prostitution in colonial Nairobi* (University of Chicago Press, Chicago, 1990); P. Geschiere, *Sorcellerie et politique en Afrique: la viande des autres* (Karthala, Paris, 1995) translated into English as *The Modernity of Witchcraft: politics and the occult in postcolonial Africa* (University Press of Virginia, Charlottesville, 1997); J.-P. Warnier, *L'Esprit d'entreprise au Cameroun* (Karthala, Paris, 1993); as well as various studies in course of publication by Filip de Boeck of the Catholic University of Leuven concerning the region of Bandundu, in Zaïre. For a discussion of Hobsbawm's theory of 'social banditry' in the context of African societies, D. Crummey (ed.), *Banditry, Rebellion and Social Protest in Africa* (James Currey, London, 1986) remains the basic work. Consultation of this volume may usefully be supplemented by the work of the Kenyan novelist Meja Mwangi.

Developments in South Africa have been studied by a rich school of social history which owes its inspiration to the work of E.P. Thompson. Particularly noteworthy is S. Marks and R. Rathbone (eds), *Industrialisation and Social Change in South Africa: African class formation, culture and consciousness, 1870–1930* (Longman, London, 1982), and C. van Onselen, *Studies in the Social and Economic History of the Witwatersrand, 1886–1914* (Longman, London, 1982). The moral ambivalence of the nationalist movement and of the struggle against apartheid is evoked in S. Marks, *The Ambiguities of Dependence in South Africa: class, nationalism and the state in twentieth century Natal* (Ravan, Johannesburg, 1986) and in S. Ellis and T. Sechaba, *Comrades against Apartheid: the ANC and the South African Communist Party in exile* (James Currey and Indiana University Press, London and Bloomington, IN, 1992). On the connections between the 'securocrats' of the National Party and crime, see S. Ellis, 'Africa and International Corruption: the strange case of South Africa and Seychelles', *African Affairs*, 95 (379) (April 1996), pp. 165–96, and, specifically on Executive Outcomes, J. Harding, 'The Mercenary Business', *London Review of Books*, 1 August 1996.

On contemporary social violence and the phenomenon of shacklords, see A. Minnaar (ed.), *Patterns of Violence: case studies of conflict in Natal* (Human Sciences Research Council, Pretoria, 1992), and J. Crush and C. Ambler (eds), *Liquor and Labour in Southern Africa* (Ohio University Press and University of Natal Press, Athens, OH and Pietermaritzburg, 1992).

In developing the concept of criminalization, we have consulted notably P. Robert, *La Question pénale* (Droz, Geneva, 1984) and 'De la "criminologie de la réaction sociale" à une sociologie pénale', *L'Année sociologique*, 31 (1981), pp. 253–83; D.F. Greenberg (ed.), *Crime and Capitalism: readings in Marxist criminology* (Temple University Press, Philadelphia, 1993); and J. Ferrell and C.R. Sanders (eds), *Cultural Criminology* (Northeastern University Press, Boston, MA, 1995).

For a comparative perspective, works which may be consulted include for example W.G. Hoskins, *The Age of Plunder: the England of Henry VIII, 1500–1547* (Longman, London, 1976); J.A. Davis and D. Ginsborg (eds), *Society and Politics in the Age of Risorgimento* (Cambridge University Press, Cambridge, 1991); M.A. Matard-Bonucci, *Histoire de la Mafia* (Complexe, Brussels, 1994); M. Cesoni, 'Développement du Mezzogiorno et criminalités: la consolidation économique des réseaux camorristes' (PhD, EHESS, Paris, 1995); S. Handelman, *Comrade Criminal: Russia's new mafiya* (Yale University Press, New Haven, CT, 1995); K. Barkey, *Bandits and Bureaucrats: the Ottoman route to state centralization* (Cornell University Press, Ithaca, NY, 1994); J. Manor, *Power, Poverty and Poison: disaster and response in an Indian city* (Sage, New Delhi, 1993); M. van Woerkens, *Le Voyageur étranglé: L'Inde des Thugs, le colonialisme et l'imaginaire* (Albin Michel, Paris, 1995); R.H. Mitchell, *Political Bribery in Japan* (University of Hawai'i Press, Honolulu, 1996); A.W. McCoy, *The Politics of Heroin: CIA complicity in the global drug trade* (Lawrence Hill Books, New York, 1991); and P. Burin des Roziers, *Cultures mafieuses: l'exemple colombien* (Stock, Paris, 1995).

Finally, we owe a great deal to the thinking of Achille Mbembe, with whom we have maintained a constant dialogue over the course of many years. Of particular importance is his book *Après la colonie*, to be published by Editions Karthala, Paris.

Austen, R.A. (1986) 'Social Bandits and Other Heroic Criminals: Western models of resistance and their relevance for Africa' in D. Crummey (ed.) *Banditry, Rebellion and Social Protest in Africa*. James Currey, London.

Barkey, B. (1994) *Bandits and Bureaucrats: the Ottoman route to state centralization*. Cornell University Press, Ithaca, NY.

Bayart, J.-F. (1990) 'L'afro-pessimisme par le bas', *Politique africaine* 40, December.

Bayart, J.-F. (1993) *The State in Africa: the politics of the belly*. Longman, London.

Bayart, J.-F. (1996) *L'Illusion identitaire*. Fayard, Paris.

Berry, S. (1993) *No Condition is Permanent: the social dynamics of agrarian change in sub-Saharan Africa*. University of Wisconsin Press, Madison, WI.

Bigo, D. (1988) *Pouvoir et obéissance en Centrafrique*. Karthala, Paris.

Bonner, P. (1993) 'The Russians on the Reef, 1947–57: urbanisation, gang warfare and ethnic mobilisation' in P. Bonner, P. Delius and D. Posel (eds) *Apartheid's Genesis*. Ravan and Witwatersrand University Press, Johannesburg.

Bottomore, T.B. and Rubel, M. (1964) *Karl Marx: selected writings on sociology and social philosophy*. McGraw-Hill, New York.

Cawthra, G. (1993) *Policing South Africa: the South African Police and the transition from apartheid*. Zed Books, London and Atlantic Heights, NJ.

Cesoni, M. (1995) 'Développement du Mezzogiorno et criminalités: la consolidation économique des réseaux camorristes'. Unpublished PhD thesis, EHESS, Paris.

Coussy, J. and Vallin, J. (eds) (1996) *Crise et population en Afrique*. CEPED, Paris.

de Boeck, F. (1998) 'Domesticating Diamonds and Dollars: identity, expenditure and sharing in southwestern Zaire' in P. Geschiere and B. Meyer (eds) 'Globalization and Identity', special number of *Development and Change* 29 (4).

Detienne, M. and Vernant, J.-P. (1974) *Les Ruses de l'intelligence. La mètis des Grecs*. Flammarion, Paris.

du Toit, A. (1993) *Understanding South African Political Violence: a new problematic?* Discussion Paper No. 43, United Nations Research Institute for Social Development, Geneva.

Ellis, S. (1994) 'Of Elephants and Men: politics and nature conservation in South Africa', *Journal of Southern African Studies* 20 (1): 53–70.

Ellis, S. (1996a) 'Africa and International Corruption: the strange case of South Africa and Seychelles', *African Affairs* 95 (379): 165–96.

Ellis, S. (1996b) 'Africa after the Cold War: new patterns of government and politics', *Development and Change* 27 (1): 1–28.

Ferrell, J. and Sanders, C.R. (eds) (1995) *Cultural Criminology*. Northeastern University Press, Boston, MA.

Freed, L. (1963) *Crime in South Africa: an integralist approach*. Juta, Cape Town.

Grégoire, E. and Labazée, P. (eds) (1993) *Grands commercants d'Afrique: logiques et pratiques d'un groupe d'hommes d'affaires contemporains*. Karthala-ORSTOM, Paris.

Guyer, J. (1995) *Money Matters: instability, values and social payments in the modern history of West African communities*. James Currey, London and Heinemann, Portsmouth, NH.

Hanlon, J. (1986) *Beggar Your Neighbours: apartheid power in Southern Africa*. James Currey and Catholic Institute for International Relations, London.

Haysom, N. (1986) *Mbangalala: the rise of right-wing vigilantes in South Africa*. Occasional Paper No. 10, Centre for Applied Legal Studies, University of the Witwatersrand, Johannesburg.

Hibou, B. (1996) *L'Afrique est-elle protectionniste? Les chemins buissonniers de la libéralisation extérieure*. Karthala, Paris.

Hoskins, W.G. (1976) *The Age of Plunder: the England of Henry VIII, 1500–1547*. Longman, London and New York.

Hutchinson, Sharon E. (1996) *Nuer Dilemmas: coping with money, war and the state*. University of California Press, Berkeley, CA.

Hyden, G. (1980) *Beyond Ujamaa in Tanzania*. Heinemann, London.

Johnson, Angela (1996) 'The Real Facts on SA Crime', *Weekly Mail & Guardian*, 7–13 June.

Kane-Berman, J. (1993) *Political Violence in South Africa*. South African Institute of Race Relations, Johannesburg.

Kopytoff, I. (ed.) (1987a) *The African Frontier*. Indiana University Press, Bloomington, IN.

Kopytoff, I. (1987b) 'The Internal African Frontier: the making of African political culture' in Kopytoff (1987a).

Kumleben, Justice M.E. (1996) *Commission of Inquiry into the Alleged Smuggling of and Illegal Trade in Ivory and Rhinoceros Horn in South Africa*. State Printer, Pretoria.

McCuen, J.J. (1966) *The Art of Counter-Revolutionary War: the strategy of counter-insurgency*. Faber & Faber, London.

MacGaffey, J. (1987) *Entrepreneurs and Parasites: the struggle for indigenous capitalism in Zaïre*. Cambridge University Press, Cambridge.

MacGaffey, J. (ed.) (1991) *The Real Economy of Zaire: the contribution of smuggling & other unofficial activities to national wealth*. James Currey, London and University of Pennsylvania Press, Philadelphia, PA.

Marchal, R. and Messiant, C. (1997) *Les Chemins de la guerre et de la paix: fins de conflit en Afrique orientale et australe*. Karthala, Paris.

Migdal, J.S. (1988) *Strong Societies and Weak States: state- society relations and state capabilities in the Third World*. Princeton University Press, Princeton, NJ.

Miller, J.C. (1988) *Way of Death: merchant capitalism and the Angolan slave trade, 1730–1830*. University of Wisconsin Press, Madison, WI and James Currey, London.

Observatoire géopolitique des drogues (1995) *Géopolitique des drogues*. La Découverte, Paris.

Paulme, D. (1976) *La Mère dévorante. Essai sur la morphologie des contes africains*. Gallimard, Paris.

Potgieter, De Wet (1995) *Contraband: South Africa and the international trade in ivory and rhino horn*. Queillerie, Cape Town.

Prins, G. and Stamp, R. (1991) *Top Guns and Toxic Whales: the environment and global security*. Earthscan, London.

Putnam, R.D. (1993) *Making Democracy Work: civic traditions in modern Italy*. Princeton University Press, Princeton, NJ.

Reno, W. (1995) *Corruption and State Politics in Sierra Leone*. Cambridge University Press, Cambridge.

Slovo, J. (1986) 'The Sabotage Campaign', *Dawn*, 25th anniversary issue.

South African Police Service (1996) *Report on the Incidence of Serious Crime During 1995*. National Crime Information Management Centre, Pretoria.

Tanzi, V. (1995) 'Corruption: arm's length relationships and markets' in G. Fiorentini and S. Peltzman (eds) *The Economics of Organised Crime*. Cambridge University Press, Cambridge.

Tilly, C. (1985) 'War Making and State Making as Organized Crime' in P.B. Evans, D. Rueschmayer and T. Skocpol (eds), *Bringing the State Back In*. Cambridge University Press, Cambridge.

van Kessel, I. (1995) ' "Beyond Our Wildest Dreams": the United Democratic Front and the transformation of South Africa'. PhD thesis, University of Leiden.

Waller, J.M. and Yasmann, V.J. (1995) 'Russia's Great Criminal Revolution: the role of the security services', *Journal of Contemporary Criminal Justice* 11 (4): 277–97.

World Bank (1995) *A Continent in Transition: sub-Saharan Africa in the mid-1990s*. World Bank, Washington, DC.